Exploring Leadership

Student Workbook

The Jossey-Bass

Higher and Adult Education Series

﹀

Exploring Leadership

v

For College Students
Who Want to
Make a Difference

Student Workbook

Wendy **Wagner**
Daniel T. **Ostick**
and **Associates**

JOSSEY-BASS
A Wiley Imprint
www.josseybass.com

Published by Jossey-Bass
A Wiley Imprint
One Montgomery Street, Suite 1200, San Francisco, CA 94104-4594—www.josseybass.com

Jossey-Bass books and products are available through most bookstores. To contact Jossey-Bass directly call our Customer Care Department within the U.S. at 800-956-7739, outside the U.S. at 317-572-3986, or fax 317-572-4002.

Wiley publishes in a variety of print and electronic formats and by print-on-demand. Some material included with standard print versions of this book may not be included in e-books or in print-on-demand. If this book refers to media such as a CD or DVD that is not included in the version you purchased, you may download this material at http://booksupport.wiley.com. For more information about Wiley products, visit www.wiley.com.

ISBN: 978-1-118-39950-7 (paper)
ISBN: 978-1-118-60250-8 (ebk.)
ISBN: 978-1-118-60251-5 (ebk.)
ISBN: 978-1-118-60252-2 (ebk.)

Printed in the United States of America
FIRST EDITION
PB Printing 10 9 8 7 6 5 4 3 2

CONTENTS

ACKNOWLEDGMENTS

Our partnerships in the development of this workbook and the facilitation guide emerged from years of collaboration and active engagement on the topic of leadership and social change. Many individuals offered expertise and input in the development of the modules and learning activities, and many others offered support and encouragement throughout the process.

Susan Komives, Nance Lucas, and Tim McMahon, the authors of *Exploring Leadership* (3rd edition), are the true architects of these materials. They provided the heavy lifting in thinking about leadership learning and personal development, and they helped us consider how to help students and leadership educators engage with their materials in powerful ways.

Thank you must go to the authors of the modules in the *Facilitation and Activity Guide*, which this workbook is based upon. These leadership educators from across the country have brought their best thinking, expertise, and experience to these materials.

Aaron Asmundson	Sean Gehrke
Mike Bishop	Stacey Guenther
Chris Bohle	Paige Haber-Curran
Kathleen Callahan	Josh Hiscock
Stephanie Chang	Eric Kaufman
Kristan Cilente	Michelle Kusel
Katherine Hershey Conlon	Nick Lennon
Dave Dessauer	Antron Mahoney
Rosanna Duran	Laura McMaster
Sarah Edwards	Steven Mills

Laura Osteen	William Smedick
Julie Owen	Meredith Smith
Jennifer Pigza	Kathryn Sturtevant
Kirstin Phelps	Paul Stonecipher
Kerry Priest	Dan Tillapaugh
David Rosch	Mark Torrez
Tom Segar	Jillian White
Melissa Shehane	Sunshine Workman

We are extraordinary thankful to our editor, Erin Null. Her critical eye, supportive voice, and listening ear gave us the thoughtful guidance necessary to address challenges and find solutions. She helped us navigate new territory with enthusiasm and wisdom, and we owe much of our success to her efforts.

Our thanks must also go to our encouraging families and friends. Their patience and support made our efforts possible, and we thank them with all our heart!

ABOUT THE AUTHORS

Wendy Wagner is an assistant professor of leadership and community engagement in New Century College at George Mason University. She is also the director of the Center for Leadership and Community Engagement and coordinator of the Leadership and Community Engagement Living Learning Community. Wendy's scholarship is related to civic engagement, leadership development for social change, and the scholarship of teaching and learning. In 2010 she received the Association of American Colleges and Universities' K. Patricia Cross Award recognizing future leaders of higher education in the areas of civic responsibility, teaching, and learning. At George Mason University, Wendy teaches courses on leadership, community based research, and community engagement. She was coeditor of *Leadership for a Better World* (2009) and the *Handbook for Student Leadership Development Programs* (2010). Wendy earned her PhD in college student personnel from the University of Maryland, her master's in college student personnel from Bowling Green State University, and her undergraduate degree in communication studies from the University of Nebraska–Lincoln.

 Daniel T. Ostick serves as the coordinator for leadership curriculum development and academic partnerships in the Adele H. Stamp Student Union–Center for Campus Life at the University of Maryland. Daniel regularly teaches coursework on leadership theory and global leadership, and has published articles and chapters on the Social Change Model of Leadership, diversity and leadership, and LGBT issues and leadership.

Prior to his current position, he held positions in residence life at the University of Maryland, the University of Texas at Austin, and the University of Illinois at Urbana–Champaign. Daniel earned his PhD in college student personnel from the University of Maryland, received his master's in college student personnel administration from Indiana University, and obtained his undergraduate degree in advertising from the University of Georgia.

INTRODUCTION

Exploring Leadership (3rd edition) defines leadership as, "a relational and ethical process of people together attempting to accomplish positive change" (Komives, Lucas, & McMahon, 2013). When leadership is approached in this way, working with others to accomplish change, everyone can be a leader. Starting with that assumption creates the opportunity for you to explore your strengths, experiences, and styles in order to engage with others in a way that feels authentic and true to you. *Exploring Leadership* addresses the important issues that emerge when leaders work with others to accomplish change through the following sections:

Understanding leadership. An overview of how leadership has been perceived differently over the years. Why modern realities call for new approaches to leadership, and the presentation of the authors' relational leadership model.

Understanding yourself and others. An exploration of your strengths, values, and ways of being in relation to others, as well as a discussion of the importance of ethics, character, and integrity.

Understanding groups and organizations. A discussion of group development and group processes and the complexity of leadership in organizations that are made up of many intersecting groups.

Understanding the nature of change and thriving together. An exploration of the processes of change and how change is influenced. How leaders can work together in ways that utilize strengths and promote well-being for all in order to have the persistence and resilience that leadership requires.

> This Workbook

This workbook contains chapter overviews, learning outcomes, activities and worksheets for engaging with the topics, and reflection questions for further exploration. Each chapter of the workbook is connected to the corresponding chapter in both *Exploring Leadership* (3rd edition) and the *Facilitation and Activity Guide*.

Charles Handy, in *The Hungry Spirit* (1999), argues that for most people life "is a process of discovery—of who we are, what we can do, and, ultimately, why we exist and what we believe. It is a circular process, because when we discover what we are capable of and work out why we exist, it changes the way we see ourselves, which can send us off in new directions, discovering new capabilities and new reasons for our existence. This spiraling journey is the true meaning of lifelong learning, and it remains, for those who pursue it, an endlessly fascinating experience, one which enriches not only the individual but all those around" (p. 223).

It is our hope that this workbook provides you with tools to engage in this process of discovery of self and others and that it leads to the enrichment of the organizations and communities you care about.

> References

Handy, C. (1999). *The hungry spirit: beyond capitalism: A quest for purpose in the modern world.* New York: Broadway Books.

Komives, S. R., Lucas, N., & McMahon, T. R. (2013). *Exploring Leadership: For College Students WHo Want to Make a Difference* (3rd edition). San Francisco: Jossey-Bass.

CHAPTER 1

An Introduction to Leadership

> Focus of Chapter

Leadership, in this text, is defined as a relational and ethical process of people together attempting to accomplish positive change. It is within this relational, ethical leadership process that everyone can be a leader. Through engaging in a critical thinking process, you can come to understand your personal experiences, strengths, and values that guide your actions as you work with others toward change.

The following are foundational principles of this emerging leadership paradigm:

- Leadership is a concern of all of us.
- Leadership is viewed and valued differently by various disciplines and cultures.
- Conventional views of leadership have changed.
- Leadership can be exhibited in many ways.
- Leadership qualities and skills can be learned and developed.
- Leadership committed to ethical action is needed to encourage change and social responsibility.

Consider these three basic principles to develop relational leadership: (1) Knowing—you must know—yourself, how change occurs, and how and why others may view things differently than you do, (2) Being—you must be—ethical, principled, authentic, open, caring, and inclusive, and (3) Doing—you must act—in socially responsible ways, consistently and congruently, as a participant in a community, and on your commitments and passions.

The study of leadership asks you to explore the "whys" of leadership. What purpose does your leadership serve? Leadership should attempt to accomplish something or change something. Leadership is purposeful and intentional. Leadership should be practiced in such a way as to be socially responsible and show a commitment to the common good.

› Learning Outcomes

- To define your currently held beliefs on the behaviors of leadership and the characteristics of a leader.
- To reflect on what you would like to know more about in the leadership process and the role of a leader.
- To assess your own skills and capacities in regards to followership competencies and to understand the influential role that followers play in supporting and defining leaders.

An Introduction to Leadership

Activity 1: Leadership Paradigm Continuum

Consider these broad statements about leaders and leadership, each reflecting different paradigms addressed in Chapter 1.

A. Leaders are born and not made.
B. I can be a leader without a formal title or position within an organization.
C. Leaders always work for good.
D. Leadership is a process of creating change.
E. Not everyone can be a leader.
F. Who I am determines how I lead.
G. If I can do it by myself it is not leadership.
H. A central component of leadership is ethics.
I. I am a leader.

On the continuum below, place the corresponding letter in the location that matches your personal beliefs about that statement:

←——→

strongly agree   strongly disagree

Questions to Consider:

What criteria did you use to decide where to place each item?

Do you think other students would agree with your assessment?

An Introduction to Leadership

Activity 2: Leaders and Leadership Behaviors

Think of a leader . . .

Now write down the actual behaviors and actions that you have observed or are aware of that
   this person engaged in which support why you believe he or she is a leader . . .

Did you have trouble moving from the first to the second question? Why? When discussing
   leader and leadership, where do we place the preponderance of our focus? On the individual or on the process? Why is this so?

What if we switched the questions?

Think of behaviors that lead you to want to work with someone . . .
Think of individuals who demonstrate these behaviors . . .
What is the difference in the approaches of the two sets of questions? What is the result in
   our responses? What is the impact on how and who we see as potential leaders?

Answer these two questions:

I believe leadership is . . .

I believe a leader is . . .

An Introduction to Leadership

Activity 3: Reflecting on Leadership

Chapter 1 states that not only will you most likely find yourself reflected in the text but also that you develop best when you are open to learning. These reflective questions are designed to assist you in the reflective process of identifying your own paradigms around leadership and what you hope to learn from this experience. Answer each question openly to give yourself a better sense of what you believe about leadership.

> "I've found that I can only change how I act if I stay aware of my beliefs and assumptions. Thoughts always reveal themselves in behavior. If we want to change our behavior, we need to notice our actions, and see if we can uncover the belief that led to the response. What caused me to behave that way and not some other way?"
>
> *Margaret Wheatley (2009, p.18)*

What beliefs motivate you to be interested in leadership?
How do you define the concepts of leader and leadership?
What actions do you notice in your relationships with others? In your group experiences?
What roles do you assume in groups?
What beliefs motivate you to assume these roles?
What kind of leader do you want to become?
My academic discipline provides me a unique lens for leadership because . . .
Role models who I learn from are . . .
My strengths are . . .
Within your relationships with others, how might you practice these strengths more?
I am guided by my core values of . . .
I stray from my values when . . .
What rituals or daily practices are important to you in your life?
When are you most likely to experience moments of learning and growth?
What recent moments have you experienced that felt truly authentic?
I am working towards . . .
I will know when I get there because . . .
As a result of participating in this leadership learning I hope to learn . . .
I have support for this learning from . . .
My first step will be . . .

An Introduction to Leadership

Activity 4: Five Follower Competencies

The text lists five competencies of followers (Exhibit 1.1):

Competency	Description
Displays loyalty	Shows deep commitment to the organization, adheres to the boss's vision and priorities, disagrees agreeably, aligns personal and organizational goals
Functions well in change-oriented environments	Serves as a change agent, demonstrates agility, moves fluidly between leading and following
Functions well on teams	Collaborates, shares credit, acts responsibly toward others
Thinks independently and critically	Dissents courageously, takes the initiative, practices self-management
Considers integrity of paramount importance	Remains trustworthy, tells the truth, maintains the highest performance standards, admits mistakes

Source: Latour & Rast (2004), p. 111. Used with permission.

Answer the following questions to explore your beliefs about followers and leadership:

- Of the five competencies, which come easiest for you when working with others? Why is that?
- Which are most difficult? Why is this so?
- As a follower, which competencies best help determine the strength of connection you have to the leader that you're working with?
- Are there any that are confusing or that you need assistance in understanding fully?

Now, write down the names of two people who think are good leaders. These can be individuals you personally know or someone in the news or in history that you consider to be a good leader.

Ask yourself how willing you would be to "follow" these leaders if given the opportunity based on the competencies. For each competency regarding each leader, consider the following questions:

Displays loyalty	How committed would you be to the organization that this individual leads? Why or why not? How well does your personal vision fit with the vision of this leader?
Functions well in change-oriented environments	What opportunities are there to shift and adapt when working with this leader? Are there opportunities to lead as well as follow?
Functions well on teams	Do you see this leader providing a team oriented environment? Are there opportunities for collaboration? Does this leader share credit with her/his team?
Thinks independently and critically	Are differences in opinion valued by this leader? What opportunities to act courageously can be rewarded by him/her?
Considers integrity of paramount importance	Does this leader generate a culture of mutual trust? How is honesty valued in this environment? What evidence is there of high performance standards?

After the individual assessment of each leader, consider these additional questions:

- Which of the competencies stick out to you as particularly important for you when working with leaders? What does this teach you about the types of leaders to look for in your personal life?
- Generally, what does this exercise teach you about the relationship between leaders and followers? How are these relationships reciprocal or even interchangeable?

› Reflection Questions for Further Exploration

- How can knowing more about leadership make you more successful in your future career or other endeavors?
- What experiences have you had that you reflected on and from which you drew a leadership lesson?
- Which of the foundational principles do you most closely agree with and why? Which is most difficult to endorse and why? Which is the most difficult to practice and why? Which is the easiest to practice and why?
- Create words that could substitute for the term follower that would have an empowering connotation to others. How do you, or would you, react to being called a follower?
- In response to the question "What is the purpose of leadership?" reflect and answer that question for yourself. What is your leadership purpose?
- What community are you associated with or do you know about that is the most involving, ethical, empowering, and inclusive? How do people in this group empower others, make decisions, elicit feedback, and share power and authority? How does this community introduce and implement change?

› References

Latour, S. M., & Rast, V. J. (2004). Dynamic followership: The prerequisite for effective leadership. *Air & Space Power Journal, 18*(4), 102–114. Retrieved April 14, 2006, from http://www.airpower.maxwell.af.mil/airchronicles/apje.html

Wheatley, M. (2009). *Turning to one another: Simple conversations to restore hope to the future.* San Francisco/London: Berrett-Koehler/McGraw-Hill.

CHAPTER 2

⌄

The Changing Nature of Leadership

◇

> Focus of Chapter

Many leadership scholars have attempted to define leadership, postulate theories, and conduct research, while others believe that all you need is common sense to understand and practice leadership. The meaning of leadership varies from one country to another and the context of leadership, or "leadership for what purpose?" is a central question in our effort to understand leadership processes.

Myths about leadership abound through time and across disciplines. The truths about leadership proposed in the text tell a different story:

- Leaders are made, not born.
- In today's fluid organizations, leadership occurs at all levels.
- Having a charismatic personality is not a prerequisite for leadership.
- There is not one identifiable right way to lead an organization or group.
- Some leaders and scholars believe it is important to make a distinction between the processes of management and leadership.
- Leadership is a discipline that is teachable.

Contemporary definitions describe leadership as a relational process based on mutual goals toward some action or change. Another common aspect of most current definitions is that there is a level of interaction between leaders and followers who are working together to accomplish a goal or some type of action, and the interaction often is based on some type of influence.

You should consider why it is important to understanding the purpose of leadership and how leadership is accomplished. The nature of leadership has changed over time, from an industrial model focused on formulas and skill sets to a post-industrial model focused on relationships and change and complexity.

Individualistic leadership theories focused on the leader, on goal achievement and assumed linear paths to change have given way to a more integrated leadership approach. These new and emerging theories give attention to the roles of every group member. A positive group process is as important as goal achievement. Problems are understood to have multiple, interrelated causes and solutions.

› Learning Outcomes

- To identify the myths and truths of relational leadership.
- To understand the historical underpinnings of the concept of leadership.
- To consider metaphorical approaches to leadership.
- To articulate how and where you recognize different leadership theories and approaches.
- To consider ways in which you see leadership approaches and theories present in your own leadership style.
- To consider which contexts emerging approaches of leadership are a good fit for you.
- To develop a foundation upon which you can truly appreciate and understand the elements of the relational leadership model.

The Changing Nature of Leadership

Activity 1: Myths About Leadership

The text describes several myths about leadership. For each myth listed below, indicate whether you strongly agree (SA), agree (A), disagree (D), or strongly disagree (SD), and answer the associated questions:

Myth 1—Leaders are born, not made.

SA   A   D   SD

- What qualities of a leader are innate and which are learned?
- Do you have leadership qualities that you have learned?

Myth 2—Leadership is hierarchical, and you need to hold a formal position (have status and power) to be considered a leader.

SA   A   D   SD

- Is there anyone you know who you would consider a leader who does not hold a formal position?
- How much easier is it to "do leadership" when you have a position?

Myth 3—You have to have charisma to be an effective leader.

SA   A   D   SD

- What does charisma mean to you?
- There are a lot of introverts—can an introvert be a good leader?

Myth 4—There is one standard way of leading.

SA   A   D   SD

- What might dictate different ways to lead?
- Do you have a standard way of leading? What is it?

Myth 5—It is impossible to be a manager and a leader at the same time.

SA   A   D   SD

- What do you think are the differences between a leader and a manager?
- How can you be more "leaderlike"?

Myth 6—You only need to have common sense to be an effective leader.

SA   A   D   SD

- Are there special skills or talents you need to be a good leader?
- How much of leading is just using common sense?

The Changing Nature of Leadership

Activity 2: Leadership Metaphors

The text explores a number of different metaphors to describe the process of leadership. These include an orchestra or symphony, a jazz band, a performing art, an episodic affair, or even the "fosbury flop." How would you describe leadership?

Leadership is like a(n) . . .

Because . . .

The Changing Nature of Leadership

Activity 3: Generations of Leadership Theories

Conceptions about the nature of leadership and who is engaged in the leadership process have changed over time. The text provides an overview of different generations of leadership theories. Review the list below (and Exhibit 2.1 in the text), and answer the questions:

Approach	Major Assumptions
Great Man	Leadership development is based on Darwinistic principles. Leaders are born, not made. Leaders have natural abilities of power and influence.
Trait	A leader has superior or endowed qualities. Certain individuals possess a natural ability to lead. Leaders have traits that differentiate them from followers.
Behavioral	There is one best way to lead. Leaders who express high concern for both people and production or consideration and structure will be effective.
Situational Contingency	Leaders act differently, depending on the situation. The situation determines who will emerge as a leader. Different leadership behaviors are required for different situations.
Influence	Leadership is an influence or social exchange process.

What would be your critique of each approach? How does this compare to the critique in the text?

Is there an approach that is more appealing to you? Why? Is there one that you do not like?

What do you think is the primary shift in approaches over time?

> Reflection Questions for Further Exploration

- Describe your personal best leadership experience—an experience in which you were most effective. What theory or metaphor best describes your leadership approach and why?
- What motivates you to take on leadership responsibilities or roles and why? Why do you lead?
- For each of the leadership theory categories (trait, behavioral, and so on), provide examples of specific leaders and participants whose leadership can be described based upon that approach. Give examples of people who practice these theories.
- Think of a real example (one you experienced or observed or from current events) that is an example of complexity leadership theory in application. Describe the relationship of the participants and leaders. How is this example different from industrial models of leadership?
- Identify an organization or community you are involved in. What would that organization look like if it was based on a shared leadership model? How might your own role be different?

CHAPTER 3

⌄

The Relational Leadership Model

◇

> Focus of Chapter

The Relational Leadership Model presents a model for you to understand leadership as a relational and ethical process of people together attempting to accomplish positive change. Relationships are the focal point of this definition with a focus on five primary components. This approach to leadership is purposeful and builds commitment toward positive purposes that are inclusive of people and diverse points of view, empowers those involved, is ethical, and recognizes that all four of these elements are accomplished by being process-oriented.

In order to practice relational leadership, you must be knowledgeable of key processes, aware of how these processes affect themselves and others, and act on this awareness and knowledge.

> Learning Outcomes

- To explore your personal conceptions of leadership and how they relate to the relational leadership model.
- To understand and apply the five components of the relational leadership model.

- To write a vision statement that supports positive change.
- To consider the role of power in the leadership process.
- To examine the definitions of the following seven concepts: ethics, integrity, values, morals, character, relationships, and conflict.
- To understand the varying definitions and understandings of leadership that exist in the world.
- To apply your understandings of leadership in a group setting.

The Relational Leadership Model

Activity 1: Reflecting on Leadership

Consider the Relational Leadership Model and its five elements.

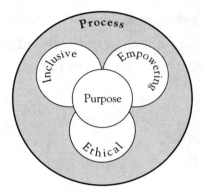

Process-oriented

Being process-oriented means that participants and the group as a whole are conscious of their process. They are reflective, challenging, collaborative, and caring. Being process-oriented means being aware of the dynamics among people in groups.

Think about a group you belong to.

- How does that group accomplish its goals?
- What interpersonal dynamics can you identify in the group? Do these hinder or help the group moving forward?

Purpose

Having a commitment to a goal or activity, collaborating and finding common ground with others.

Think about a group of which you are a member. This could be a student organization, sports team, residential community, team of coworkers, or any other group to which you belong. Answer the following questions:

- What is the purpose/vision of your group?
- Do other members of your group know this vision? Can they articulate it?
- How can you ensure buy-in to this purpose?

Empowering

A sense of self-claiming ownership and expecting to be involved; creating an environment that promotes participation.

Think of a time when you felt empowered in a group and a time when you did not feel empowered in a group.

- How did these two experiences affect your ability to interact within the group?
- What was the difference in group leadership and context between those two times?

Inclusive

Understanding, valuing, and actively engaging diversity in group, including differing views, approaches, styles, and aspects of individuality.

Answer the following questions:

- Have you ever witnessed exclusion in a group? What were the consequences of this exclusion?
- What could have changed in the group to ensure inclusion was practiced?

Ethical

Leadership is driven by values and standards. Relational leadership is moral in nature and involves leading by example.

List 15–20 values you feel define you as an individual.

Now, of those values, identify the 10 values that you consider to be more important, or core, to you as an individual. Write them below.

Now, of those 10 values, identify the three or four values that you consider to be the most important, or core, to you as an individual. Write them below.

Answer the following questions:

- Was it easy or difficult to settle on your core values?
- How might you identify core values of the groups you belong to?
- How often might values conflicts occur in groups?

The Relational Leadership Model

Activity 2: Develop a Vision Based on Values

This is an opportunity for you to develop a vision statement from scratch based on your operational and end values. End values are essential conceptualizations of what the future would look like or ultimate goals of an organization such as freedom, health, or equality. Operational values are those values the organization believes are essential or important to achieve the established end goals, for example honesty, loyalty, or compassion.

Think of an organization you could develop (for example, a student organization, nonprofit organization, or neighborhood association) and then designate three end and three operational values for that organization.

Based on those values, develop a purposeful vision statement that promotes positive change. Remember the other elements of the Relational Leadership Model in the development of the vision statement.

Reflect on the experience with these questions:

- How and why did you come up with the values you did? Do you feel any values are missing or overlooked?
- Did you feel the final vision statement reflected the values you established?
- How would you feel about working for an organization with that vision statement?

The Relational Leadership Model

Activity 3: Connecting Ethics to Leadership

"Good" leadership often has two meanings: (1) good, meaning "effective" or successful at reaching the goal and (2) good, meaning "moral." However, the text implies that for leaders to be effective, they must *also* be moral.

Ethical decision making requires:

- Knowledge of one's own values as well as the values of one's group
- An understanding of what is moral within the context of the situation
- Strength of character
- An ability to build strong relationships
- Competence in navigating conflict

Consider the following definitions for terms associated with ethical leadership:

- *Ethics*—principles or standards governing behavior of an individual or organization
- *Integrity*—acting consistently according to a firmly established character pattern; "doing the right thing"
- *Values*—core beliefs that guide an individual's thoughts or actions based on the ends he or she desires
- *Morals*—guidelines arising from one's conscience in discerning good from evil
- *Character*—the overall mark of a person's words and actions, determined from long-term behavior; quality of honesty and courage
- *Relationships*—emotional connections between people
- *Conflict*—an incompatibility or quarrel between parties, ideas, or goals

Provide an example or two of what each term "looks like" in action.

- Ethics

- Integrity

- Values

- Morals

- Character

- Relationships

- Conflict

The Relational Leadership Model

Activity 4: Concept Map for Ethics and Leadership

A concept map is simply a visual representation of the relationships between concepts, just as a map in an atlas is a visual representation of relationships between geographic places. Many people use concept maps to help understand or explain how complex concepts interact with one another in practice.

An example of a concept map (that describes a concept map) is here:

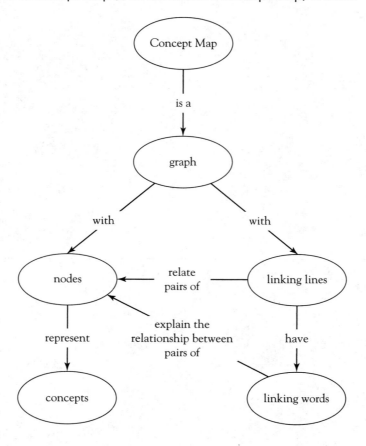

Create your own unique concept map of how ethics, integrity, values, morals, character, relationships, and conflict are in tangible relationship with each other to create ethical leadership.

If you are struggling, ask yourself the following questions:

- Is one concept more central to ethical leadership than the others? If so, how?
- Is there a concept that should be ''on top'' or ''on the bottom?''
- Can someone have integrity without ethics and values?
- How do conflict and relationships affect a leader's character?

The Relational Leadership Model

Activity 5: Personal Reflection on Ethics

Answer these two questions:

What is the most difficult part about leading ethically for you? Why?

How might you utilize others to help you grow as an ethical leader?

The Relational Leadership Model

Activity 6: Bases of Power

Exhibit 3.2 in the text explains French and Raven's six bases of power, as follows:

Type	Definition
Reward	The person can deliver positive consequences or remove negative consequences.
Coercive	The person can deliver negative consequences or remove positive consequences.
Legitimate	Group members believe the person ought to have power because of his or her position or responsibilities.
Reference	Group members do what the person wants out of respect, liking, and wanting to be liked.
Expert	Group members believe the person has a special knowledge or skill and is trustworthy.
Informational	Group members believe the person has useful knowledge not available elsewhere.

Adapted from Johnson & Johnson (2006), p. 237.

You may intentionally use some sources of power, but others may attribute some sources of power *to* you without you knowing what is happening. Power is present in all leadership processes, and it is important for you to consider where you have power and how you use it.

Using the chart below, consider each source of power and write down an example of when you have either used or been given power for each. You may find that you can easily come up with examples for some and cannot come up with examples for others. What does this tell you about how you use or receive power?

Type	Examples
Reward	
Coercive	
Legitimate	
Reference	
Expert	
Informational	

❯ Reflection Questions for Further Exploration

- Think of a leader whom you would consider to be a role model, someone who practices what he or she preaches and lives by high standards. Think of local, national, or historical exemplars. What is it about the role model you identified that qualifies that person as an exemplary leader? What values does he or she profess, and what practices does he or she consistently live by?
- Describe your leadership compass. What principles or ethics guide your personal life and your leadership?
- Identify a situation in which you successfully used one or more of French and Raven's sources of power. What contributed to your effective use of each of those sources of power? Think of an example of a leader who abused one of these sources of power. What were the consequences of that person's leadership?
- As you review the five elements of this Relational Leadership Model, which are most comfortable for you and why? Which involve knowledge, skills, or attitudes that you have not yet learned or developed?
- In their simplicity, models often omit concepts that could have been included. What concepts would you add to any of the five elements of this model, or what new elements do you think should be included?

❯ Reference

Johnson, D. W., & Johnson, F. P. (2006). *Joining together: Group theory and group skills* (9th ed). Boston, MA: Allyn & Bacon.

CHAPTER 4

Understanding Yourself

> ## Focus of Chapter

Self-awareness is critical to effective leadership. An important part of self-awareness is developing a deeper understanding of your natural talents and strengths, how to practice and build upon them, and how to use them to achieve your goals. In this pursuit, self-reflection can be one of the best and most essential leadership development tools you have.

It is also important to consider the ways in which your individual background and relationships have influenced the development of particular talent in different ways; you may have had more opportunity to practice and develop some talents, whereas some of your talents may be working against you if you are not practicing how to use them effectively.

> ## Learning Outcomes

- To be able to identify personal stories that exemplify your talents and strengths.
- To create a personal vision or "philosophy" statement that encompasses your strengths, values, and beliefs.

- To reflect on the ways your talents manifest in your daily life and how these talents can be leveraged to accomplish goals.
- To explore and discuss the ways in which your top talents interact with and influence one another, and learn about the similarities and differences in the ways talents manifest differently in different people.
- To think about nontalents or talents in "overdrive," and identify potential complementary partners in your life who can help manage these areas.
- To consider how your character strengths are reflected in your practice of leadership.
- To identify the essential skills associated with successfully leading change and your competency regarding each skill.

Understanding Yourself

Activity 1: Understanding Your Talents

The first step in developing your talents into true strengths is becoming aware of the ways in which you are already using them. Additionally, in order to continue building your capacity to use your talents effectively, you must practice using them intentionally.

After you have completed the Clifton StrengthsQuest assessment (an individual one-use code is available in the print and e-book editions of *Exploring Leadership,* 3rd edition, or you can purchase a code from https://www.gallupstrengthscenter.com/Purchase/) and have read the definitions of your top five talents, answer the following questions about each of your talents:

Talent 1:

What does this talent mean to you? How would you describe this talent to someone else in your own words?

When was the last time you used this talent?

What is a goal you have for yourself? How can you use this talent to help you reach your goal?

What are three ways in which you can practice using this talent in the next week?

Talent 2:

What does this talent mean to you? How would you describe this talent to someone else in your own words?

When was the last time you used this talent?

What is a goal you have for yourself? How can you use this talent to help you reach your goal?

What are three ways in which you can practice using this talent in the next week?

Talent 3:

What does this talent mean to you? How would you describe this talent to someone else in your own words?

When was the last time you used this talent?

What is a goal you have for yourself? How can you use this talent to help you reach your
goal?

What are three ways in which you can practice using this talent in the next week?

Talent 4:

What does this talent mean to you? How would you describe this talent to someone else in
your own words?

When was the last time you used this talent?

What is a goal you have for yourself? How can you use this talent to help you reach your
goal?

What are three ways in which you can practice using this talent in the next week?

Talent 5:

What does this talent mean to you? How would you describe this talent to someone else in your own words?

When was the last time you used this talent?

What is a goal you have for yourself? How can you use this talent to help you reach your goal?

What are three ways in which you can practice using this talent in the next week?

Understanding Yourself

Activity 2: Talents in Action

Two people with any of the same talents in their top five could still behave very differently. This is due in part to the different contexts within which people are raised. It is also because each of your top five talents interact with the other four, influencing your behavior in a variety of different ways.

Consider the ways in which your top five talents interact with one another and draw or create a visual representation of your "talents in action." Here are some prompting questions to get you started:

How do your talents interact with one another?

How do these interactions show up in your day-to-day behavior?

Are there times when some talents show up more than others?

What do your talents allow you to do?

Understanding Yourself

Activity 3: What about Weaknesses?

A "weakness" can either be an area of "nontalent" *or* one of our talents "in overdrive." When a talent is in overdrive, it is being used ineffectively and in an extreme way that is not helpful. A few examples:

Empathy in overdrive can lead someone to be perceived as a pushover.
Command in overdrive can lead someone to be perceived as overly bossy.
Futuristic in overdrive can lead someone to be perceived as unrealistic.

Pick two of your top five talents and reflect on the following questions:

Talent:

What does this talent look like in overdrive?

How can you leverage your *other* talents to manage this more effectively?

Think of a person in your life who has a different and complimentary talent. How might she or he be able to help you recognize when you are in overdrive?

Talent:

What does this talent look like in overdrive?

How can you leverage your *other* talents to manage this more effectively?

Think of a person in your life who has a different and complimentary talent. How might she or he be able to help you recognize when you are in overdrive?

Understanding Yourself

Activity 4: Values in Action (VIA) Exploration

After you have completed the Values in Action (VIA) Survey (available free at www.viacharacter.org), you will receive a report that identifies your top character strengths, giving you greater insights into what makes you who you are.

The VIA classification scheme includes 24 character strengths, organized around these six virtues (Peterson & Seligman, 2004):

- Courage—"doing what is right, even when one has much to lose" (p. 36)
- Justice—fairness; citizenship; equity
- Wisdom and knowledge—"intelligence hard fought for, and then used for good . . . noble intelligence—in the presence of which no one is resentful and everyone is appreciative" (p. 39).
- Humanity—showing generosity and being altruistic; exhibiting prosocial behaviors such as kindness and benevolence
- Temperance—the ability to monitor and manage emotions; showing self-control
- Transcendence—having a connection to someone higher than oneself that inspires hope, awe, and gratitude; achieving meaning and purpose beyond self-interest

Of the 24 strengths, list your top 10 character strengths below:

What virtues do these 10 strengths represent?

How do you feel you actively live these strengths and virtues?

How do these strengths show up in how you interact in groups and organizations? How have you exercised these strengths in the past week?

Understanding Yourself

Activity 5: Personal Vision Statement

Imagine that it is five years from now, what do you want to be able to say about your life? Here are some reflection questions that might help you dream:

What do you see as the connection between your signature strengths themes and core values?
What future do you want to be able to say you lived?
What do you want your friends to say about you? Your coworkers? Your community? Those that are marginalized? Your life partner?

In a simple phrase, write a powerful statement that describes what you want to be. There is not really a "right" way to do this other than it feels right to you. When you look at it, does your body tingle? Do you feel excited and full of joy when you read it? Does it pull you forward? Some people write vision statements about the outer world (what you would see, hear, or do) and others write one concerning the inner world (your thoughts, emotions, and feelings). Do what makes sense to you.

Understanding Yourself

Activity 6: Leading Change Skills Self-Assessment

Part of personal development involves the identification of skills and the acquisition of knowledge necessary to effectively exercise leadership in a variety of different settings. Use this self-assessment to become familiar with different areas of leadership skill development (self development, interpersonal development, team development, organizational and group development, and transitional development) and to assess your personal level of competence in each area.

Please circle the number you feel best represents your current skill level for each item.

6—you feel you are fully competent with nothing left to develop and if called upon, can effectively teach others

5—you are very competent and that others' learning increases as a result of working with you

4—you feel competent and that you can use this skill in various situations effectively

3—you are somewhat competent and you are applying and practicing and improving as you gain more experience

2—you recognize the skill as essential and are purposefully gaining the knowledge and information to understand

1—you are beginning to gain the knowledge

Self-Development

Developing perspectives, insight, and understanding about ourselves is something we are often too busy to do. We may not even know how to go about doing it. Self-development has two main dimensions: *self-awareness* and *self-management*.

- Developing *self-awareness* involves assessing your own strengths, weaknesses, values, motivations, passions, and your own leadership style. It helps you verbalize and prioritize what is important to you.
- Developing *self-management* skills involves learning about your own sense of integrity, initiative, accountability, adaptability, goal setting, and wellness. It teaches you to stop and reflect on how you view things.

My assessment of my own skill level and knowledge pertaining to self-awareness is

1   2   3   4   5   6

My assessment of my own skill level and knowledge pertaining to self-management is

1   2   3   4   5   6

Interpersonal Development

These are skills that will help you build better relationships with everyone you interact with at work, at home, and in your community. Interpersonal development has four main dimensions: *relationship building, communication, ethical practices*, and *team development*.

- Developing *relationship building* skills involves improving your ability to be empathetic, inclusive, impartial, and fair. It also stresses the importance of trust in relationship building.
- Developing *communication skills* is about learning how to listen. It is about effectively communicating within cultures and between cultures in nonverbal, verbal, and written formats.
- Developing *ethical practices* will build your awareness and ability to empower people and use your own power in positive ways. It will improve your decision-making and help you exert influence in synergistic ways, as well as teach you the importance of integrity in fostering and maintaining interpersonal relationships.
- *Team development* emphasizes building critical skills for use in team environments such as facilitation, collaboration, conflict resolution, followership, compromise, and assessing group dynamics.

My assessment of my own skill level and knowledge pertaining to *relationship building* is

1   2   3   4   5   6

My assessment of my own skill level and knowledge pertaining to *communication skills* is

1   2   3   4   5   6

My assessment of my own skill level and knowledge pertaining to *ethical practices* is

1   2   3   4   5   6

My assessment of my own skill level and knowledge pertaining to *team development* is

1   2   3   4   5   6

Organizational and Group Development

Organizational and group development has four main dimensions: leading change, project and program effectiveness, system thinking, and community building.

- Developing skills in *leading change* is critical to your future as well as the future of others. We live in a dynamic world that demands skills such as visioning, creativity, risk-taking, personal resiliency, and modeling in everything we do. We all recognize the value of leading change rather than being left behind.
- Developing skills in *project and program effectiveness* are vital to the success of any organization. It is vital to develop your ability to organize, budget, plan, delegate, and continuously improve. Because organizations are made up of people, it is important to recognize accomplishment, celebrate success, retain valuable human assets, document progress, and assess the impact of variables that affect your organization.
- Developing *systems thinking* skills can enhance your ability to analyze the complexity of organizational environments. It can also help you develop perspectives in critical thinking and build competencies in assessing the effect of environmental factors on your organization. It can help you understand how politics play a part in organizational contexts and even show you how to use technology.
- Developing *community building* skills is inherent to any organization, because every organization is a community of people. It is important to learn more about citizenship, cultural understanding, and coalition building.

My assessment of my own skill level and knowledge pertaining to *leading change* is

1   2   3   4   5   6

My assessment of my own skill level and knowledge pertaining to *project and program effectiveness* is

1   2   3   4   5   6

My assessment of my own skill level and knowledge pertaining to *systems thinking* is

1   2   3   4   5   6

My assessment of my own skill level and knowledge pertaining to *community building* skills is

1   2   3   4   5   6

Transitional Development

Transitions happen continuously throughout our lives. Graduating from college. Getting a job. Building a career. Getting involved in clubs, organizations, and civic groups. Discovering new places, people, and ideas. Transitions you plan for and stuff that just happens unexpectedly.

Transitional leadership has only one dimension—*Sustaining leadership*. Developing sustaining leadership skills will help you realize your goals. More important, it will help others reach their goals.

* *Sustaining leadership* is about networking with others and making sure that perpetual learning is available to all of us. It is about coaching, developing others, and mentoring. It is about sharing experiences, knowledge, and insight.

My assessment of my own skill level and knowledge pertaining to *sustaining leadership* is

1   2   3   4   5   6

Source: Allen, Julian, Stern, & Walborn. *Future perfect: A guide for professional development and competence* (1987).

> Reflection Questions for Further Exploration

- Write your own personal mission statement. What is your purpose in life? What values are important to you? What do you want to be? What attributes and capabilities are important to you?

- Think about all the behaviors you do currently in your leadership or membership role. Which ones are you doing that are in your top strengths? Which ones are not? How can you bring your strengths into better alignment with your leadership?

- Think of a good act or gesture you did within the last 24 hours. Think of three additional good deeds. Reflect on what you did that enriched someone's life, whether it was a small or large gesture. Now think of someone who has helped you in your lifetime. Appreciate that person's kindness and impact on you—what are you most grateful for? Think of a challenging moment or encounter you have experienced recently. Can you picture yourself transcending the problem? Are you able to experience equanimity? (Salzburg, 2011).

> References

Allen, K. E., Julian, F. H., Stern, C. M., & Walborn, N. C. (1987). *Future perfect: A guide for professional development and competence.* Columbia, SC: NACA Educational Foundation.

Peterson, C. & Seligman, M.E.P. (2004). *Character strengths and virtues: A handbook and classification.* New York, NY: Oxford University Press.

Salzburg, S. (2011). *Real happiness: The power of meditation.* New York, NY: Workman Publishing.

CHAPTER 5

Understanding Others

> Focus of Chapter

It is essential for you to engage in awareness-building around personal identity as a pre-requisite to better understand the identities and background experiences of others. Through the reflective process of identifying the "self," the "other," and the commonalities and differences that exist between the two, you can enhance your ability to build a multicultural mindset and engage in perspective-taking, the ability to examine situations or ideas through alternate perceptions of reality.

Gender roles have historically enforced traditional notions of how one should behave. From a young age, people are socialized to act in accordance with these expected gender roles. Many facets of society, such as family, culture, and media, reinforce gender roles related to being "tough" or "nurturing." Narrowly defined gender roles can limit both men and women and influence the ways men and women feel they need to lead and the expectations of how others should lead.

Leadership is, in part, navigating and understanding the diversity of groups, organizations, and cultures. Exploring other characteristics such as ethnicity and culture will enhance your intrapersonal and interpersonal leadership capacities. Culture is a broad term that involves a group's shared thoughts, feelings, symbols, and behaviors. It is essential for you to understand and appreciate difference, as well as develop the skills necessary to lead and communicate with diverse groups and increase your multicultural competence to engage others in an inclusive and empowering leadership process.

> Learning Outcomes

- To identify multiple facets of social identity.
- To consider how gender roles limit both men and women in leadership and to discern the value of masculine and feminine approaches to leadership.
- To deepen your awareness of cultural assumptions held about others.
- To consider the importance of strengthening and enhancing cultural knowledge and to identify how cultural influences are relevant to leadership skills and knowledge.
- To understand and articulate awareness of intercultural sensitivity.
- To identify and explore various ways to address sensitive multicultural challenges.
- To apply inclusive communication techniques.

Understanding Others

Activity 1: Understanding the Complexity of Identity

Part One: Please list or describe various parts of your social identity:

Ability:

Gender:

Nationality:

Race/Ethnicity:

Religious affiliation:

Sexual orientation:

Socioeconomic status/Class:

Other aspects of your identity that are important to you? List here.

Part Two: Please reflect on the following questions or statements:

Which of my identities do I think about most frequently? Why might that be? What do I generally think about when it's on my mind?

Describe a situation in which one or more of your facets of social identity influenced your behavior in the situation or reaction to the situation.

Describe one or more facets of your social identity in which you feel misunderstood or stereotyped.

Understanding Others

Activity 2: Gender Influences on Leadership

List 5–10 gender norms or stereotypes for women in our society:

List 5–10 gender norms or stereotypes for men in our society:

Consider these questions:

- What are your reactions to these lists? Do you agree with any of them? Do you think others would have similar words or different words?
- Where have you heard or seen some of these gender roles and stereotypes depicted or reinforced in society?
- Have you had anyone you respect challenge these stereotypes?

Now, finish these sentences:

"Female leaders should . . ."

"Male leaders should ..."

Given the gender norms and stereotypes that you generated already, what are some attitudes, behaviors, or skills that you feel are expected for male and female leaders?

Explore the following questions in more detail:

- What examples do you have of men or women who confirm or disconfirm the attitudes, behaviors, and skills we generated?
- Are there any of these attitudes, behaviors, or skills that are strictly gendered, meaning only men or only women are capable of possessing them?
- Which of these attitudes, behaviors, and skills do you believe contribute to effective leadership?

Understanding Others

Activity 3: Cultural Influences on Leadership

Create an illustration that symbolizes your background. You might include items such as family traditions, vacations, celebrations, or memories. What might you share if someone asked about your background?

Respond to the following questions:

- Was creating this drawing challenging for you? Why or why not?
- How do you decide what to share or not share with other individuals?
- If you are in a group with someone else doing this worksheet, compare your drawings and think about what your differences or similarities in backgrounds say about you.

Understanding Others

Activity 4: Case Studies of Unassertive, Assertive, and Aggressive Communication

For each scenario below, consider what an unassertive, an assertive, and an aggressive response would be:

Scenario 1: You are involved in a student organization that wants to organize a Christmas party before winter break. You notice that not everyone identifies as Christian, and you recommend having a general holiday party, instead of focusing specifically on a Christmas-themed party. Another student leader says, "It doesn't really matter too much, because we always have a Christmas party, and if someone doesn't want to attend, they don't have to." The group proceeds to discuss buying a Christmas tree, food options, gift exchange plans, popular Christmas music to play, etc. How would you handle this situation?

Unassertive response:
Even though you have several ideas, you reply
   almost meekly. You deny your own rights
   and are intimidated. You may feel trapped
   or afraid to speak up. You are fairly passive.

Assertive response:
This response acknowledges that the other
   person had every right to have an opinion,
   and you have a right to make your own
   decisions.
Being assertive means you can share your
   opinion without feeling guilty or without
   apologizing.

Aggressive response:
This response denies the other person has any
   rights and is rarely appropriate.

Scenario 2: You are part of a group that plans a large-scale service event in the community. This event typically involves physical labor. You are in charge of recruiting and coordinating all volunteers. One volunteer sends you an email sharing that he is a new student on campus and is really excited to participate in the event this year. He also shares that he is in a wheelchair and will need special accommodations in order to participate. While your email is open, another student reads the email and says, "Oh, don't worry about that. Just tell him that this event involves physical activity, so he won't be able to participate. He should understand." How would you handle this situation?

Unassertive response:
Even though you have several ideas, you reply
   almost meekly. You deny your own rights
   and are intimidated. You may feel trapped
   or afraid to speak up. You are fairly passive.

Assertive response:
This response acknowledges that the other
   person had every right to have an opinion,
   and you have a right to make your own
   decisions.
Being assertive means you can share your
   opinion without feeling guilty or without
   apologizing.

Aggressive response:
This response denies the other person has any
   rights and is rarely appropriate.

    Scenario 3: You are the treasurer for a student organization. After making an announcement at a meeting about paying dues, $40.00, several students come up to you asking for an extension, or the option of a payment plan. They share that they are not in a financial state to pay up front, but would really like to continue their involvement with the organization. You decide on a payment plan and all is well. The next day, another student leader informs you that for the committee retreat, everyone needs to pay $100.00 within three days to pay for all up front costs. If students are unable to do so, they will not be allowed to attend. You share with that individual the situation regarding the students who were unable to pay dues, and the student says, "That's not my problem. Ask them just to borrow money from their parents, or they can't go." How would you handle this situation?

Unassertive response:
Even though you have several ideas, you reply
 almost meekly. You deny your own rights
 and are intimidated. You may feel trapped
 or afraid to speak up. You are fairly passive.

- -

Assertive response:
This response acknowledges that the other
 person had every right to have an opinion,
 and you have a right to make your own
 decisions.
Being assertive means you can share your
 opinion without feeling guilty or without
 apologizing.

- -

Aggressive response:
This response denies the other person has any
 rights and is rarely appropriate.

Scenario 4: During one of your organization's retreats, you play an icebreaker game that involves female members "quizzing" male members about the things they find attractive about the opposite sex, and vice versa. For example, a male will get in the middle of the circle and the female members will shout questions about dating, relationships, and so forth regarding the opposite sex.

 This game is somewhat of a tradition for this organization and every year the questions get more and more personal. You know a few of the new members identify as gay and lesbian. When you approach another student leader about your discomfort putting students who identify as gay and lesbian in a potentially oppressive environment, their response is, "It's just a game. It really isn't that big of a deal and this one game shouldn't really matter." How would you handle this situation?

Unassertive response:

Even though you have several ideas, you reply
   almost meekly. You deny your own rights
   and are intimidated. You may feel trapped
   or afraid to speak up. You are fairly passive.

Assertive response:

This response acknowledges that the other
   person had every right to have an opinion,
   and you have a right to make your own
   decisions.

Being assertive means you can share your
   opinion without feeling guilty or without
   apologizing.

Aggressive response:

This response denies the other person has any
   rights and is rarely appropriate.

› Reflection Questions for Further Exploration

- How are your communication, conflict-resolution, and decision-making behaviors or tendencies influenced by your perceptions of the gender, race, ethnicity, family practices, or other characteristics of others in the group?
- Ask a friend who is different from you to take you to an event or gathering at which the majority of others will be like your friend. What is easiest and hardest for you to understand about the practices in that group? Which of your own characteristics make it hardest for you to gain this understanding?

CHAPTER 6

Leading with Integrity

> Focus of Chapter

An exploration of ethics and integrity is central to the conversation about leadership practice. It is important to develop skills to create and sustain ethical organizational environments, to analyze the moral dimensions of transforming leadership theory, and to examine the ethical influences that you and other participants have on organizations through behavior modeling. You are encouraged to consider the aspects of bad leadership, the perils of having ethical lapses, and the importance of moral courage in practicing ethical leadership.

There are eight assumptions about leadership for you to explore:

1. Ethics is the heart of leadership.
2. All leadership is values-driven.
3. Personal values intersect with organizational values.
4. Ethical leadership can be learned.
5. Ethical leadership involves a connection between ethical thought and action.
6. Character development is an essential ingredient of ethical leadership.

7. Ethical leadership is a shared process.
8. Everything we do teaches.

Ethics exist in a cultural and temporal context. What is considered ethical in one culture or time period may be different for another culture or at a different time. Some authors have asserted that there are common ethical values across cultures, such as love, truthfulness, fairness, freedom, unity, tolerance, responsibility, and respect for life. Others have suggested that there are common virtues, such as wisdom and knowledge, courage, love, and humanity, justice, temperance, and spirituality and transcendence.

You make decisions about what is right or wrong, good or bad, every day. Ethical leaders should stop to reflect on how ethical decisions are made. You need to understand diverse viewpoints and empower other individuals and groups to behave ethically. Ethical decision-making models are discussed which can help you move beyond self-interest, to consider other individuals, groups and the world as a whole.

› Learning Outcomes

- To analyze and interpret the core purpose of your student organization(s).
- To engage in effective values-based decision making.
- To identify your own assumptions about leadership and compare these to the text and other students.
- To consider cultural dimensions of leadership in relationship to personal culture.
- To articulate how you currently make decisions about what is ethical or unethical.
- To consider alternative ways of making ethical decisions through reflection, listening and discussion.
- To apply ethical theories to various ethical scenarios.

Leading with Integrity

Activity 1: Values Continuum

Mark each item below on a scale of 1–4, with 1 meaning Strongly Agree, 2 meaning Agree, 3 meaning Disagree and 4 meaning Strongly Disagree.

It is OK for one student organization to violate a university policy when many other student organizations do the same without any consequences.

It is OK to lie to organization members if telling the truth would hurt the members' feelings.

It is OK to withhold information from university staff if you think it might be used against you.

It is OK to make exceptions to officer qualifications in the effort to elect the most desirable candidate for a position.

It is OK to speak negatively about another group because that group spoke negatively about yours.

It is OK to not hold members accountable for irresponsible actions as long as those actions don't happen "all the time."

It is OK to advertise using public relations materials that are disruptive and degrading.

It is OK to commit to an event and then not attend because you are "busy."

It is OK to allow your friends to break the rules.

Kidder (1995) provides three principles for ethical decision making (pp. 24–25):

- *Ends-based thinking:* Philosophers refer to this as utilitarianism, best known by the maxim, *Do whatever produces the greatest good for the greatest number*. Based on cost-benefit analysis, determining who will be hurt and how helped. At the heart of this principle is an assessment of consequences, a forecasting of outcomes.

- *Rule-based thinking:* Kant's "*categorical imperative:* follow only the principle that you want everyone else to follow." Ask yourself, "If everyone in the world followed this rule of action I am following, would that create the greatest good or the greatest worth of character?" Rule-based thinking is based firmly on duty—what we ought to do rather than what we think might work. This is deontological thinking, meaning "obligation" or "duty."

- *Care-based thinking:* putting love for others first. The Golden Rule is an example of care-based thinking—*do to others what you would like them to do to you.* Care-based thinking puts the feature of "reversibility" into play: test your actions by putting yourself in another's shoes and imagining how it would feel if you were the recipient, rather than the perpetrator, of your actions.

Using these three principles, place letters in the right column of the table above—an E (for ends-based thinking), an R (for rules-based thinking) or a C (for care-based thinking) for the approach you took to decide each item.

Which letter did you use most to decide if a behavior was ethical? Do you think this represents how you usually approach ethical decision making?

Leading with Integrity

Activity 2: Ethical Assumptions about Leadership

Respond to the following questions regarding assumptions about ethics:

Assumption 1—Leadership can be "good" even if it isn't ethical.

- Do you usually think of ethics when you discuss leadership, or do you focus more on results, outcomes, and effectiveness?
- Is leadership better when it's ethical? Are ethics *more* important than outcomes?

Assumption 2—Leadership can be value-neutral.

- What kinds of leadership might be value-neutral?
- Do you use ethics at all times? Can you be ethics-neutral or do you always carry a point of view?

Assumption 3—It's OK if your personal values don't align with your organization.

- What impact does non-alignment have on you? On your organization?
- How can you find out if an organization has values that match yours?
- Does everyone in an organization need to agree on what is ethical?

Assumption 4—People cannot learn to be more ethical.

- Do you have an example of a time when you learned from doing something unethical?
- When is the last time you discussed ethics with friends? Family? Anyone?
- Can you learn ethics on your own?

Assumption 5—You can be ethical and do unethical things.

- "But I am a good person" and "My actions don't define me" are sometimes said to show this contrast. How tied are ethics to actions?
- When have you been faced with an ethical choice?

Assumption 6—You must walk the talk.

- Do you know anyone you don't think is ethical? What impact does that have on your relationship? If in an organization, what impact does it have on the organization?

Assumption 7—Ethics are most powerful when given to an organization by its positional leader.

- In your groups, do you ever talk about the groups' ethical values or statements?
- Who is responsible for making sure members of a group are ethical? How do they do this?

Assumption 8—People will understand if I do something unethical if it's for good reasons.

- Some espouse the "newspaper rule" to determine ethical behavior—how would you feel if your actions were printed in your hometown newspaper? Do you think this is a fair measure?
- "Everyone else does it" is sometimes said to justify behaviors. Have you been a part of an organization where unethical behavior has seeped into the organization?

Leading with Integrity

Activity 3: Ethical Decision Making

Decision making is something that people do not always engage in with conscious thought. This activity is designed to uncover your often subconscious rational for ethical decisions.

Mark each item below on a scale of 1–4, with 1 meaning Strongly Agree, 2 meaning Agree, 3 meaning Disagree and 4 meaning Strongly Disagree.

Try your best to choose based on what *you* honestly feel you would most likely *do* in the situations. As you respond, identify what the competing values in this decision are for you and think about what reasoning you used to choose between the competing values.

I just signed an honor code pledge agreeing to abide by academic honesty policies, including any witnessing of cheating incidents. My best friend is in my accounting course and I observed that friend cheating during an in-class exam. I would report my friend.

I am taking care of my friend's cat while my friend is on vacation. One day, about halfway into my friend's vacation, I walk into my friend's place to discover that his pet cat has died. I would wait until my friend got back from the trip to tell him.

My friend is joining a student organization and I know she is being hazed, but the friend asks me not to tell. I would still tell someone who could have an impact on stopping the hazing.

If I saw a homeless person begging on the street, I would give him money.

If a good friend just bought an expensive outfit and asks me if I like it (and I think it's awful) I would share my true feelings with that friend.

I would purchase tickets to a concert that I had no interest in so that I can sell them online for a profit.

I would continue to eat chicken if I knew that the chicken I was eating came from a farm that had horrible, but sanitary, conditions for the animals.

I would speak up if I heard someone that I do not know make an offensive ethnic slur at a party.

If I discover that a good friend is cheating on his or her partner and I am also very close to that partner, I would tell that partner about my discovery of the affair.

I have been waiting for about 8 minutes in a long line of traffic during rush hour, waiting to merge onto another street. A car pulls up next to me and the driver has their blinker on, trying to get over into my lane. I would allow the driver to pull in front of me.

Some additional questions to consider:

- What statements/situations were more emotional for you? Why?
- What surprised you about this activity?
- Were there any patterns to your decisions?
- Do you think there are items that you would differ in your score from most people?
- How does this exercise relate to being a student?
- How does this exercise relate to leadership?

Leading with Integrity

Activity 4: Organizational Ethical Audit

Ethics are not just about what you and your organization values. It is also about how those values are enacted daily through relationships, processes, and decision making. Think about an organization in which you are currently a member and answer the following questions.

How would you describe the ethical climate in this organization?

What does the organization do to encourage members to do what is right?

What does the organization do that may encourage inappropriate behavior?

What happens when someone violates the ethical standards of the organization?

How could the organization become more supportive of ethical behavior?

List the ways you could reward ethical behavior in your organization. Develop an action plan to put these ideas into place.

> Reflection Questions for Further Exploration

- Think of a national, historical, or local person who you believe is an ethical leader. What skills, behaviors, attitudes, or characteristics does that person exhibit? Think of a national, historical, or local person who you believe is an unethical leader—a person who practices bad or toxic leadership. What skills, behaviors, attitudes, or characteristics does that person exhibit? How have both leaders' behaviors influenced or impacted followers or others in the organization?
- Think of a person who has served as a role model to you. Why did you choose that person? What skills, behaviors, attitudes, or characteristics does that person exhibit?
- How can or do you serve as a role model to others in your group or community?
- Identify an ethical dilemma you faced in which there were two competing values such as honesty and loyalty. How did you work through that dilemma and what was the outcome. What, if anything, would you do differently if you could go back in time to that same situation?
- Identify an organization or institution you believe has a strong commitment to ethics. How would you describe that organization? How do the members and leaders of that organization create and sustain an ethical organizational environment? How do they model ethical behaviors? How can you apply these lesson to your organization?

> Reference

Kidder, R. M. (1995). *How good people make tough choices: Resolving the dilemmas of ethical living*. New York, NY: Fireside.

CHAPTER 7

Being in Communities

> Focus of Chapter

In college and university life, you are likely involved in many different communities, from organizations you join, communities you live in, and sports in which you participate. Why are these communities important to you and what makes them effective? Gardner (1990) outlines eight elements that define effective communities: (1) wholeness incorporating diversity, (2) a shared culture, (3) good internal communication, (4) caring, trust, and teamwork, (5) group maintenance and governance, (6) participation and shared leadership tasks, (7) development of young people (or new members), and (8) links with the outside world.

All organizations, indeterminate of their goals, engage in a similar developmental process that moves through stages towards an authentic community. It is important to make clear that it is not the end that is most important, but instead the process of achieving those ends. Most groups will start out as a pseudo-community and while some might progress to the other stages, potentially landing within authenticity, it is also just as likely that some groups may remain in the initial stage, unable or unwilling to continue.

Principles of community building that you can engage in to become more effective members of their community include being committed, being mindful about what you do and say, being unconditionally accepting of others, being concerned for both yourself and others, seeking to understand others as completely as possible, being ethical, and being peaceful (Gudykunst, 1991). These principles assert that members who are dedicated and practice community-building skills will enrich the organization.

› Learning Outcomes

- To consider how privilege influences your life and the communities you belong to.
- To relate theory to practice through personal experiences.
- To articulate the differences between communities you belong to that are effective and those that are not.
- To identify your own communities and how you can contribute to them.
- To understand the challenges and opportunities created within community building.

Being in Communities

Activity 1: Privilege "Walk"

Diversity is a major component of community and it is important for you to be able to explore the topic. Privilege and diversity impact communities and how you form your world view and experiences. This activity will help you understand that privilege plays an important role in community.

This activity is typically done with a group of students, facilitated by a trained educator. But, for the purposes of exploring the concept of privilege, can also be done individually. It can be powerful to share your results with another individual and discuss the similarities and differences in your results.

Read each statement and give yourself points according to the directions:

If your primary ethnic identity is American (from the United States), give yourself one point.

If your parents are or were professionals: doctors, lawyers, give yourself one point.

If you attended private school or summer camp, give yourself one point.

If you were ever called names because of your race, class, ethnicity, gender, or sexual orientation, give yourself minus one point.

If you were taken to art galleries or plays by your parents, give yourself one point.

If your place of work or school is closed on your major religious holidays, give yourself one point.

If you had to rely primarily on public transportation, give yourself minus one point.

If you can openly show affection for your partner without fear of harassment or assault, give yourself one point.

If you saw members of your race, ethnic group, gender or sexual orientation portrayed on television in degrading roles, give yourself minus one point.

If you can go to a clothing store and find clothes in your size easily, give yourself one point.

If your first language is spoken in most places you go, give yourself one point.

If your dietary needs are met at most public locations, give yourself one point.

If you were ever afraid of violence because of your race, ethnicity, gender or sexual orientation, give yourself minus one point.

If you ever inherited money or property, give yourself one point.

If your parents did not grow up in the United States, give yourself minus one point.

If you are a Christian, give yourself one point.

If your parents or family told you could be anything you wanted to be, give yourself one point.

If you ever had to skip a meal or were hungry because there was not enough money to buy food when you were growing up, give yourself minus one point.

If you do not have to worry where curb cuts are located because you are able-bodied, give yourself one point.

If your ancestors were forced to come to the United States not by choice, give yourself minus one point.

If growing up you had more than 100 books at home, give yourself one point.

If you never have to worry about having enough money to have food on the table, give yourself one point.

If you were ever ashamed or embarrassed of your clothes, house, or car, give yourself minus one point.

If you studied the culture of your ancestors in elementary school, give yourself one point.

If you ever tried to change your appearance, mannerisms, or behavior to avoid being judged or ridiculed, give yourself minus one point.

If you were told that you were smart and capable by your parents, give yourself one point.

If you are rarely seen as a sex object in the media, give yourself one point.

What is your final score?

Consider these questions:

- Were there any statements that surprised you or made you uncomfortable?
- What types of privilege and diversity were parts of this activity? Was anything missing?
- Did some of the statements feel unfair? How did it feel have a higher or lower score?
- How does this relate to privilege and diversity in your communities (college, city/town, state, nation, and world communities)?
- How can you use these differences and privileges to benefit others in your community?

(Modified from multiple diversity and privilege resources from Winthrop University Diversity Manual and Colorado State University Human Issues Programming)

Being in Communities

Activity 2: Effective Communities

Identify two communities you belong to (one effective and one not effective). Now, review Gardner's (1990) eight elements that define effective communities and comment on how each organization does or does not realize these elements.

	Organization 1	Organization 2
Wholeness incorporating diversity		
A shared culture		
Good internal communication		
Caring, trust, and teamwork		
Group maintenance and governance		
Participation and shared leadership tasks		
Development of young people (or new members)		
Links with the outside world		

Now that you have thought about how the organizations do or do not practice these elements, answer the following questions:

- Why do you think this is?
- Is the community still effective?
- Could it be effective? How?

> Reflection Questions for Further Exploration

- Describe a community of which you were an active member. Try to relate this community to the four stages of community development as outlined by Peck. Did you experience each stage? If not, why not? What was each one like? How were they similar? How were they different?

- To what degree is some kind of community awareness essential for the Relational Leadership Model? Can the model still be a helpful frame to guide your leadership role (as a participant or as a positional leader), even if a sense of community does not exist in your groups or organizations?

- Think about a healthy community that you are or were associated with and identify its characteristics. Now think about a community you know of that is unhealthy or is in the early stages of community development. What has contributed to the status of this community? How would you go about strengthening this community?

- Communities sometimes are strengthened during times of crisis. Provide an example not already mentioned in the chapter of a community in crisis that became stronger as a result.

> References

Gardner, J. W. (1990). *On leadership*. New York, NY: Free Press.

Gudykunst, W. B. (1991). *Bridging differences: Effective intergroup communication*. Thousand Oaks, CA: Sage.

CHAPTER 8

Interacting in Teams and Groups

❯ Focus of Chapter

You have likely been a part of or interacted in some sort of group. Reflecting upon how groups form and develop over time will help you navigate your roles within group settings. Group dynamics include such processes as how the group makes decisions, how the group handles its conflict, and how the group meets its leadership needs. Group roles and group norms are the driving influences of group dynamics. Groups depend on two kinds of roles: group-building roles (actions that focus on the relationships among members) and task roles (focus on accomplishing the purposes of the group).

Group norms are the rules of conduct that lead to consistent practices in a group. Some norms are explicit and clearly seen by all participants. Other norms may have evolved through the cultural practices of the group. The group norms collectively contribute to the group's overall personality.

Conflict, a natural process within a group, can serve your groups well when handled skillfully. Conflict helps groups clarify values and arrive at better, more creative solutions. Win-win outcomes typically result from healthy collaboration and communication whereas win-lose and lose-lose outcomes always result in marginalization and exclusion.

While decision making is not always a group process, as a group leader, you should consider if decisions support the group's vision and mission, what opinions group members have about the issue, whether the decision will heighten or limit involvement, if the decision is ethical and principled, and if you should slow down making the decision so that others can get involved.

> Learning Outcomes

- To explore stages of group development.
- To apply both group-building roles and task roles in a group activity.
- To consider how group norms impact the functioning of teams and group.
- To understand how different types of conflict arise in groups and consider several strategies to handle group conflicts effectively.
- To understand the pros and cons of different approaches to group decision making.
- To apply the consensus model of group decision making.

Interacting in Teams and Groups

Activity 1: Tuckman's Touch Points

Reflect about a group in which you currently are a member. Of Tuckman's stages of group development, described in detail in Chapter 8, which one best represents that group at the present time? Forming, storming, norming, or performing?

Current stage of group:

What are key components of this stage?

What challenges have you observed due to being in this stage?

What victories have you experienced or do you hope to experience in this stage?

What strategies might you see assisting the members of this group to proceed to the next stage?

Interacting in Teams and Groups

Activity 2: Adjourning and the Role of the Leader

The Adjourning stage of group development can easily get overlooked especially with groups who have a fixed term and have high turnover in officers from year to year. Groups often select new officers and begin the group development process all over again each year. Unfortunately, missing that time at the end of the cycle to thoughtfully move through the adjourning stage is a mistake many organizations make.

Read over the following scenario and answer the listed questions:

You are a member of a service organization that contributes 10,000 hours of service per year as an organization to local nonprofits in your town. Each year the group selects new officers in April, which leaves little time for them to transition. Your group has never fully moved through the adjourning stage of group development as an executive team or organization.

Your task is to develop a plan that would help this organization move through the adjourning stage.

How can members take time to pause and make meaning of the experience they have had together?

How can members be recognized?

How can the executive team explore what they have learned over the course of the year?

What other stakeholders should be involved in this stage?

How will you celebrate their success?

How can you apply these lessons to an organization *you* are involved in?

Interacting in Teams and Groups

Activity 3: Experience with Group Norms

Identify at least one organization with which you are familiar. Answer the following questions:

How would you describe the personality of the organization?
- Is it more relationship or task-oriented?
- Are there multiple levels and layers of leadership, or is it a more open structure?

How does the organization articulate rules of conduct?
- Does it have bylaws or published meeting procedures?
- Is there an orientation for new members?

For group norms that are not clearly articulated, how do members know about them?
- How are guests or new members introduced to the organization?
- What cues for accepted behavior are visible at organizational meetings?

Interacting in Teams and Groups

Activity 4: Hieroglyphics

Using the space below, think about the norms of your organization and draw them in the form of hieroglyphics (i.e., cave-type drawings). Think of these hieroglyphics like road signs, directing new members how to proceed and what to watch for.

Interacting in Teams and Groups

Activity 5: Drawing Conflict

This activity is meant to have you reflect upon your experiences in dealing with conflicts that arise when involved in a group (i.e., sports team, student organization, group project).

Using the space below, draw an interpretation of what that conflict felt like for you. Consider what your natural inclination was in how to manage that conflict. Represent that pictorially.

If you were to show another person this drawing and ask for their interpretation (without you offering any explanation), what do you think they would notice?

Some questions for you to answer:

- What is your natural instinct for dealing with conflict within a group?
- When you were drawing your experience with conflict, how easily did you get brought back into that experience? How do you think that specific experience might play into similar experiences in the future?

Interacting in Teams and Groups

Activity 6: Behavior-Feelings-Reason

Consider the Behavior-Feelings-Reason (BFR) model of dealing with conflict, seen here:

When you [name the behavior], I feel [state the feeling or emotion] because [provide the reason].

For each item below, think about how you might address this conflict using the Behavior-Feelings-Reason model. Write a sentence and ideas for how you might handle each scenario:

Conflict: Your roommate has been watching the television or listening to music very loudly at night when you would like to be sleeping causing some frustration lately.

BFR Approach:

Conflict: You loaned your friend some money a month ago to pay off some of their bills and she or he has not paid you back yet.

BFR Approach:

Conflict: You overheard your friend talking badly about you recently to another friend.

BFR Approach:

Conflict: Your teammate has been really negative about the team's string of losses lately, and it has started to affect the team's morale.

BFR Approach:

Conflict: Your group member is not following through on their obligations as well as not meeting the group's imposed deadlines.

BFR Approach:

Conflict: A member of your student organization has a personal issue with another member of your team and that is having an impact on the group's overall effectiveness.

BFR Approach:

Now, think of a conflict you have seen or been a part of in one of your groups or organizations. Write the conflict below and how you would handle it using a BFR approach.

Conflict:

BFR Approach:

Conflict:

BFR Approach:

Interacting in Teams and Groups

Activity 7: Group Decision-Making Approaches

Exploring Leadership briefly outlines Johnson and Johnson's (2006) seven methods of decision making, as follows: (1) decision by authority without discussion, (2) expert member, (3) average members' opinions, (4) decision by authority after discussion, (5) minority control, (6) majority control, and (7) consensus. Answer the following questions for each approach:

Decision by authority without discussion

What does this method mean?

What are the strengths of this approach?

What are the weaknesses of this approach?

When and why have you used this approach?

Decision by expert member

What does this method mean?

What are the strengths of this approach?

What are the weaknesses of this approach?

When and why have you used this approach?

Average members' opinions

What does this method mean?

What are the strengths of this approach?

What are the weaknesses of this approach?

When and why have you used this approach?

Decision by authority after discussion

What does this method mean?

What are the strengths of this approach?

What are the weaknesses of this approach?

When and why have you used this approach?

Minority control of decision

What does this method mean?

What are the strengths of this approach?

What are the weaknesses of this approach?

When and why have you used this approach?

Majority control of decision

What does this method mean?

What are the strengths of this approach?

What are the weaknesses of this approach?

When and why have you used this approach?

Decision by consensus of group

What does this method mean?

What are the strengths of this approach?

What are the weaknesses of this approach?

When and why have you used this approach?

Interacting in Teams and Groups

Activity 8: Roles in Teams and Groups

This activity provides an exploration of the typical group roles that affect group dynamics and process.

For each scenario listed below, pick *one* of the group roles listed and answer the questions included.

Group Roles (pick one for each scenario)

- Group Maintenance
  Focused on group dynamics especially the relationships demonstrated among group members. This role focuses on the needs of other group members and is attentive to creating harmony among them.
- Task
  Focused on accomplishing the purpose of the group, including giving information and opinions and moving the group along by summarizing and by using various decision-making strategies. This role is focused on completing the scenario efficiently and within the allotted time frame.
- Special Interest Pleader
  Focused on pushing their point like a broken record. People in this role try to prevent the group from moving on when they are not getting their way.
- Blocker
  Focused on resisting or blocking any group action by being negative and disagreeable about everything. Feel free to use phrases such as "this is unproductive" or "I don't agree with that statement."
- Active Member
  Focused on being actively engaged through listening and supporting the group decision-making process. This role should speak when something important needs to be stated but should not dominate the discussion.
- Nonparticipant
  Focused on other things outside of what the group is working on and does not event listen or engage other members of the group in anyway. This role may text, update social media status to "most boring meeting ever," and mumble verbally "I don't know why I'm here."

- Observer
  Focused on recording the interactions between the group members. This role should try to identify the other roles in the group. Observer should not speak unless spoken to directly.

Scenario 1

Your organization is planning to bring a speaker to campus who exemplifies the values of your organization such as integrity and hard work. You've narrowed the invite list down to two speakers in your organization's price range. Speaker one is a notable TV personality best identified with their exploits on a popular reality show. Speaker two is a retired news anchor with a long resume of awards for journalistic integrity.

Your chosen role (pick from list above):

How might this role act in this scenario?

Have you even seen someone in this role? Have you ever been this role in a group?

Scenario 2

You are on an executive board for a large student group on-campus. Your group has struggled to get general members to attend group meetings. Your next general meeting is critical because if you lose any more involved members, your group may no longer be eligible for funding through your university's club requirements.

Your chosen role (pick from list above):

How might this role act in this scenario?

Have you even seen someone in this role? Have you ever been this role in a group?

Scenario 3

Your student group is reevaluating its marketing strategies for the coming semester due to lack of attendance at programs and meetings. General members have expressed concerns about the amount of paper used on-campus and their lack of attention to the over abundance of email and social media messages.

Your chosen role (pick from list above):

How might this role act in this scenario?

Have you even seen someone in this role? Have you ever been this role in a group?

Scenario 4

Your group is attempting to plan its first ever service project. There are three local non-profit organizations that are interested in hosting your group. Nonprofit one organizes local park cleanup and beautification projects for Saturday mornings. Nonprofit two is a local soup kitchen that serves dinner at 8 P.M. on Friday nights. Nonprofit three is an afterschool tutoring program that requires volunteers to be paired with a few local elementary school students and work with those students for an entire semester.

Your chosen role (pick from list above):

How might this role act in this scenario?

Have you even seen someone in this role? Have you ever been this role in a group?

Additional Questions to Answer

Is there a group role you play most often? Least often? Why?

Does the role you play change depending on the group? Why or why not?

What have you previously observed from others about what actions or statements helped the discussion move forward or hindered group processes?

What advise might you give other individuals when they encounter each role?

Interacting in Teams and Groups

Activity 9: Team Action Toolkit

This activity will provide you with experience in applying the Relational Leadership Model to case studies based upon examples in the text.

Consider each item listed below as a "tool" your group can use to move through a group process. For each listed scenario, consider which tools would be the most effective to use.

Tools to Consider

- *Creative Conflict* includes setting ground rules for group discussions, disagreeing with civility and ensuring that everyone's voice is heard.
- *Group Decision Making* puts emphasis on mission/vision based decisions, checking in with group members to hear opinions, understanding who should be involved in the decision making process and how they should be involved. Additionally decisions should be ethical, and should be made knowing the group's expectations in the decision making process.
- *Teams and Teamwork* relates to group morale, motivation, support of each other, common purpose, diversity of roles, inclusion of others, sense of group identity and interdependence of group members.
- *Goal Setting* is all about establishing group trust, and creating SMART goals (Specific Measurable Attainable Relevant Time-bound goals).
- *Team Learning* occurs through dialogue of personal experiences, values and stories, as well as collective listening, reflection, and thought.
- *Individual Leadership* involves serving as a facilitator for team learning. One must reflect on their own personal motivations, advocate for others, and reflect on group process and outcomes.
- *Team Leadership* consists of team members feeling valued, teams that are effective in achieving the goals they set out to accomplish, and a careful balance between monitoring, taking action, and paying attention.
- *Create Your Own:* A tool or item not here, create your own (e.g., ask your advisor).

Scenario 1

Students in STEM had a very concerning last meeting with only three members present. They are a month away from what is supposed to be a large celebration in honor of their 100th anniversary as an organization. Early on in the semester, there was a lot of excitement and group energy toward the celebration. The group leader led several brainstorming sessions until consensus was reach that the celebration should be a campuswide concert.

In the next meeting however, the group was informed that a concert would be logistically out of their budget range and was asked to brainstorm again what type of celebration should take place. At this point, many members were confused and began to question their purpose in being at the meeting and the purpose of the organization.

Using your toolkit, what opportunities for group development were missed during the past several meetings of students in STEM?

If you were a member of this organization what would you have done differently?

If you were a student in this group, how would you utilize the toolkit after only three members attended your last meeting?

Scenario 2

The Business Entrepreneurs Club (BEC) is locked in a fierce debate over what activities the organization should engage in. Robert is a new member at his first meeting. He notices that the group meeting consists of one continuous argument where members are debating whether to design a logo for boxer shorts and use the profits to host a party or design a T-Shirt to raise money for a local recreational charity. The group meeting seems incredibly divided with two subgroups competing for attention and ultimately the final say on what activities the BEC should engage in. Robert is unsure of whether he will show up for another meeting.

Using your toolkit, what tools would be helpful for BEC to reach some sort of consensus?

If you are Robert, at your first meeting, what are your initial reactions to the espoused mission of the group and the actual actions of the group?

Scenario 3

The Black Student Union (BSU), a once strong organization on campus recently decided to vote itself out of existence due to dwindling attendance at social events and lack of interest. Several members of the group met up and reformed a new group called Umoja (meaning Unity) with a new purpose aimed at being inclusive of all students on-campus, and providing wide ranged events including social, educational and advocacy events for campus. Recently, the Umoja leadership team was approached by a group of BSU alumni donors wondering the reasons why BSU was no longer in existence. Umoja is currently crafting a response to the alumni group.

Using the toolkit, why do you think BSU took a bold step of disassembling?
What tools did the new Umoja demonstrate in their actions and what would be a good response to the BSU alumni group?

> Reflection Questions for Further Exploration

- Think about your personal style in conflict situations. Now read the descriptions that follow and assign a percentage to each conflict style based on how often you use it. Your total percentages should add up to 100%.
  - Style 1: I avoid conflict and stay away from issues involving conflict.
  - Style 2: I want to be the winner in conflict situations.
  - Style 3: I want to be liked, so I avoid conflict.
  - Style 4: I believe in compromise.
  - Style 5: I view conflict as an opportunity to identify and solve problems.
  - What are the advantages and disadvantages of each style? Consider your most preferred styles and identify circumstances in which these styles are most and least effective for you.
- Think of the best team of which you have ever been a member. This could be any kind of team (newspaper staff, student government, club or organization, scouts, 4-H, sports team). What made this team special? Was there ever a time when this team had to learn something? Describe that experience.
- Identify a group or team you that you are involved in and have the most experience. Turn to Exhibit 8.5 in *Exploring Leadership* and highlight the strengths you believe are most prominent in this group. How can you work as a team to more effectively maximize everyone's and your strengths?

> References

Johnson, D. W., & Johnson, F. P. (2006). *Joining together: Group theory and group skills* (9th ed). Boston, MA: Allyn & Bacon.

Tuckman, B. W. (1965). Developmental sequence in small groups. *Psychological Bulletin, 63,* 384–399.

Tuckman, B. W., & Jensen, M. C. (1977). Stages of small group development revisited. *Group and Organizational Studies, 2,* 419–427.

CHAPTER 9

Understanding Complex Organizations

> Focus of Chapter

Reflect on the diverse perspectives that makes up an organization and how mission, vision and values can be a common tie in challenging situations. You should understand why your organization functions, what is its purpose, and broadly speaking, what is the relevance for the greater community. You and other members within an organization should be encouraged to question the "way things have always been done" to look at innovative approaches to increase the effectiveness of the organization. You should also continually explore how you recruit and invite collaborative partnerships that celebrate the diversity of your campus community.

Complex organizations have influence—they influence the life and learning of members within the organization, and influence people and groups outside of the organization through network interactions. The more you understand the culture, connections, and cycles of organizations, the greater your ability to encourage all members to take an active role in accomplishing organizational goals. The best organizations are those in which members are continually learning and growing in order to stay relevant and adapt to new challenges.

> Learning Outcomes

- To understand the systemic nature of organizations.
- To be able to analyze a complex organization and consider the role of leadership within a complex organization.
- To identify and describe aspects of organizational culture.
- To understand the role leaders play in creating organizational culture.
- To apply concepts of organizational learning to your own organizations.
- To identify and describe aspects of organizational culture and to understand the role leaders play in creating organizational culture.
- To apply concepts of organizational learning to your own organizations.

Understanding Complex Organizations

Activity 1: Flipping the Pyramid

One way of reconceptualizing an organization is to flip the traditional pyramid upside down so that the members are at the top and the president is at the bottom (see Figure 9.2 in the *Exploring Leadership* text). This reconceptualization means that the work of the president is to support the efforts of the other officers and committee chairs so they can better meet the needs and wishes of the members.

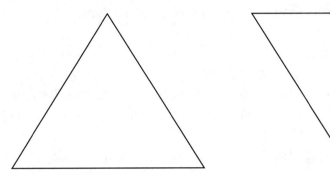

Turn your organizational pyramid upside down. How well does your leadership help the other members of the organization work toward achieving the purposes for which the organization exists? Who are your members, and what are you as a leader doing to meet their wants and needs? How are you using the talents of your members?

Understanding Complex Organizations

Activity 2: Organizational Analysis

Select a complex organization to analyze (most likely one you do *not* belong to). A complex organization as an entity of more than 20 people comprised of groups of groups that exist to achieve a specific purpose. Conduct an internet search of websites, wikis or blogs related to your chosen organization to analyze available information on the organization purpose, structure, culture, and operations.

Use the following questions to thoroughly analyze the organization:

Mission: Why does this organization exist?

Vision: What is the ideal future for this organization?

Core Values: What actions or beliefs guide action and behavior in this organization?

Size: How large is the organization? How many people are part of, or work for, this organization? How is the organization structured?

Culture: What can be inferred about the organization's culture from the information collected?

Operation: Why can this organization be considered complex? How does this organization operate? Where does it operate? How does it work to achieve its stated purpose? Are there any factors that increase the complexity of this organization's operation?

Now, answer the following questions:

- Would you want to be a member/employee of this organization? Why or why not?
- How are the structure, function, and culture of an organization impacted by its mission?
- What role does leadership play in a complex organization?
- What do you think is the most essential component of an organization?

Understanding Complex Organizations

Activity 3: Campus Culture Survey

Consider the following scenario:

> Your friend is a high school senior who is considering coming to your college or university next year. When they come to campus for a visit, you volunteer to accompany them on the campus tour and orientation activities of the day. During the tour, you begin to notice some cues and clues of the campus culture.

> Make observations about the campus culture by answering the following questions:

- What do you physically "see" while on a campus visit?
- What are the structures and processes of the campus that are visible?
- What values seem to be important to your school?
- What do students hear about or see during their visit that communicates ideals, goals, values, and aspirations of the school?
- Who are considered role models around here? Whose actions are recognized and rewarded for high standards of performance?
- What are the formal or informal guidelines for "how life works" around here? Are there certain ways people dress, talk, or act?
- What might be some of the underlying assumptions that drive the values and actions of the school (of faculty, staff, or current students?)

    Try to create a "campus recruitment brochure" for your campus that outlines or illustrates the key aspects of campus culture. What would you include?

Understanding Complex Organizations

Activity 4: Enhancing Organizational Learning

The text (see Exhibit 9.4 and below) lists ways leaders can enhance organizational learning (adapted from Yukl, 2009, p. 50). Using this list, identify the organization in which you are *most* involved and answer the included questions:

Encourage people to question traditional methods and look for innovative new approaches that will be more effective.

- When was the last time your organization openly asked for new ideas from its members?
- Are most of your programs or initiatives ones you have done before? Why?

Articulate an inspiring vision to gain support for innovative changes from members of the organization.

- What is the vision for your organization? Would everyone be able to articulate it?

Encourage and facilitate the acquisition of skills needed for collective learning by individuals and teams.

- When was the last time your organization purposely taught its members a new skill?
- How often do you share new information with other members?

Strengthen values consistent with learning from experience and openness to new knowledge, thereby helping to create a learning culture in the organization.

- When something needs to get done, how often is that task done by someone who has done it before?
- Does your organization have a method of training new members?

Encourage social networks that will facilitate knowledge sharing, collaborative development of creative ideas, and the acquisition of political support for innovations.

- How does your organization share knowledge electronically? Is there a repository for multiple members to access?
- How many members of the organization are typically involved in decision making?

Help people recognize when important learning has occurred and to understand the implications for the team or organization. Encourage teams to conduct after-activity reviews to identify effective and ineffective processes.

- After your last program or initiative, did you organization formally discuss the process and what you learned?
- For your program or initiatives, do you often discuss past experiences prior to planning?

Encourage people to acknowledge when a new initiative is failing and should be aborted rather than continuing to waste resources on it.

- Do you feel comfortable sharing your opinion if an initiative is failing?

Develop, implement, and support programs and systems that will encourage and reward the discovery of new knowledge and its diffusion and application in the organization.

- When someone in your organization has a new idea, how hard is it to have that idea considered?
- Does your organization often consider multiple points of view or do a few voices dominate the discussion?

Review your answers to these questions. Do you feel like your organization is actively committed to learning? Why or why not? How might your group commit to becoming a learning organization?

Understanding Complex Organizations

Activity 5: The Five Whys

Consider this imaginary conversation with the chair of a campus entertainment committee:

Why does your organization exist?	To provide campus entertainment for students.
Why is that important?	So they'll have something to do and have fun.
Why is that important?	So they'll enjoy going to school here and stay out of trouble.
Why is that important?	If they like going to school here and stay out of trouble, they'll stay in school and hopefully graduate.
Why is that important?	If they graduate, hopefully they'll go out and be successful, make a big salary, and contribute money to the school.
So you really work for the Development Office?	I guess so!

Source: Adapted from Ross (1994), pp. 108–112. Used with permission of Rick Ross.

Now, apply this to one of the organizations you belong to:

Why does your organization exist?

Why is that important?

Why is that important?

Why is that important?

Why is that important?

> Reflection Questions for Further Exploration

- Find your organization's mission statement. Does it meet the criteria suggested by Jones and Kahaner? What are your statement's strengths? Where does it fall short? How could you change it to make it more reflective of both the purpose and the personality of your organization? How compelling is it?
- Reflect for a couple of minutes on the core values of your organization. Write down what these values are. Do not worry about the number you have, but try to come up with at least ten. Do not worry about putting them into any order. Once you have your list, pick the top five—the five most important core values. Again, do not worry about prioritizing your choices. From this list of five, pick the three most important values. Finally, pick the most important core value for your organization. How well does this list match the list of your personal values?
- Think about the concept of multicultural organizational development. How committed is your organization to full participation by members of all cultural and social groups? How committed is your organization to ending all forms of social oppression that might exist within the organization? What could you do to increase this commitment?
- How virtual is your organization? How do you use technology to interact? If you use technology in your organization, how do you use it? What has been the effect of its use? What have been the benefits and challenges associated with its use?

> References

Ross, R. (1994). The five whys. In P. M. Senge, A. Kleiner, C. Roberts, R. Ross, & B. Smith (Eds.), *The fifth discipline fieldbook: Strategies and tools for building a learning organization* (pp. 108–112). New York, NY: Currency/Doubleday.

Yukl, G. A. (2009). Leading organizational learning: Reflections on theory and research. *The Leadership Quarterly, 20,* 49–53.

CHAPTER 10

Understanding Change

◇

> Focus of Chapter

Different types of change and the scope of a change can invoke a variety of individual responses. A change can be a small adjustment or a deep, transformational experience that reframes your organizational values and practices. Individual responses to change vary and the model of individual reactions to change depends upon whether this change was perceived to be positive or negative. Change may occur slowly over time or suddenly, like when something reaches a "tipping point" and becomes widespread very quickly. In order to facilitate change in an organization, you must understand how individuals experience change and how you manage yourself during a transition.

For any lasting change to occur, you, as a leader, must help group members move beyond what is comfortable and embrace the risk of the unknown. Just as individuals do, organizations must feel a compelling sense of need in order to embrace the sometimes painful change process.

> Learning Outcomes

- To understand the stages an individual experiences during a change process.
- To consider your own response to change and how you can be well suited for change experiences.
- To understand the complex nature of leading organizational change.
- To consider what risks the organization is and is not willing to take in pursuit of change.
- To apply Kotter's Eight-Stage Process of Creating Major Change to organizational change goals.
- To identify (or envision) something personal or organizationally that if changed will create a positive outcome.
- To understand five planning areas to consider for successfully leading change.
- To develop an implementation plan for leading change for your identified change item.

Understanding Change

Activity 1: Personal Change Inventory

In order to facilitate organizational change, you need to understand change from the individual perspective. Schlossberg identifies four potential resources for managing change: the situation, yourself, supports, and strategies for coping. One way for you to understand how you manage change is take an inventory of how you have responded to change in the past.

Think of a significant personal change that occurred in your life and write that here:

Now, respond to the following questions regarding the change you identified:

- What happened?
- How did you feel?
- What past experiences were you able to draw on to help you navigate this change?
- What people or resources were useful?
- What coping strategies did you utilize?
- What phases did you go through in order for this change to become a part of your life?

Explore this further with the following questions:

- What did you observe about how you manage change?
- What similar phases did you experience as part of your change?
- What sources of support did you identify that aided you in making the change?
- Looking ahead, how might these resources be useful in making future changes?

Understanding Change

Activity 2: Change Quotations

For each quote below, consider what that quote says about leadership and change.

- "The world as we have created it is a process of our thinking. It cannot be changed without changing our thinking."—Albert Einstein
- "If you want change, you have to make it. If we want progress we have to drive it."—Susan Rice
- "They always say time changes things, but you actually have to change them yourself."—Andy Warhol
- "Sometimes good things fall apart so better things can fall together."—Marilyn Monroe
- "He who rejects change is the architect of decay. The only human institution which rejects progress is the cemetery."—Harold Wilson
- "It's not that some people have willpower and some don't. It's that some people are ready to change and others are not."—James Gordon
- "There is nothing like returning to a place that remains unchanged to find the ways in which you yourself have altered."—Nelson Mandela
- "Change your thoughts and you change your world."—Norman Vincent Peale
- "Man cannot discover new oceans unless he has the courage to lose sight of the shore."—Andre Gide
- "In a chronically leaking boat, energy devoted to changing vessels is more productive than energy devoted to patching leaks."—Warren Buffett

Place a star next to the two that most closely represent how you feel about change. Place an X next to the two that least represent your feelings about change. What does this tell you about how you approach change in your groups and organizations?

Understanding Change

Activity 3: Stages of Change and the Relational Leadership Model

Exhibit 10.1 in the text connects Kotter and Cohen's (2002) Eight Steps for Large-Scale Change and relates them to the Relational Leadership Model. For each step listed below, conduct a personal assessment and think of a time you have been engaged in change and exercised these actions.

Step	Action	New Behavior
1	Increase urgency	People start telling each other, "Let's go, we need to change things!" (RLM—Purpose)
2	Build the guiding team	A group powerful enough to guide a big change is formed, and they start to work together well (RLM—Inclusive, Process)
3	Get the vision right	The guiding team develops the right vision and strategy for the change effort (RLM—Purpose and Ethical)
4	Communicate for buy-in	People begin to buy into the change, and this shows in their behavior (RLM—Purpose)
5	Empower action	More people feel able to act, and do act, on the vision (RLM—Empowering)
6	Create short-term wins	Momentum builds as people try to fulfill the vision, while fewer and fewer resist change (RLM—Process)
7	Don't let up	People make wave after wave of changes until the vision is fulfilled (RLM—Purpose)
8	Make change stick	New and winning behavior continues despite the pull of tradition, turnover of change leaders, and the like (RLM—Process)

Which of these actions have you engaged in?

Which of these actions have you *not* engaged in? Why not?

> Reflection Questions for Further Exploration

- What are some obstacles you might face in facilitating change? What are some reasons why some people are resistant to change?
- Think of an experience in which a successful change effort took place. What factors in the organization or community environment led to successful change? What did the leaders and members do to prepare for change efforts? How were people aligned with the change?
- Why is it important for organizations to be flexible and open to change? What happens to organizations that are resistant to change?
- What are the root causes of inertia in organizations?
- Why is it that some ideas or behaviors or products start epidemics and others don't? What can you do to start a social epidemic of your own?

> Reference

Kotter, J. P., & Cohen, D. S. (2002). *The heart of change: Real-life stories of how people change their organizations.* Boston, MA: Harvard Business School Press.

CHAPTER 11

Strategies for Change

> ## Focus of Chapter

The exploration of values is essential for creating positive social change as you work at the individual, group, and society or community levels. The Social Change Model emphasizes the reciprocal, interconnected dynamic of three perspective levels. Individual values are consciousness of self, congruence and commitment. Group values are controversy with civility, common purpose, and collaboration. The societal value is citizenship.

The model incorporates the following key assumptions: (1) Leadership involves effecting change for the greater good, (2) leadership is a collaborative and relational process, (3) leadership is value-focused, (4) all students are potential leaders; not just those who hold formal positions, and (5) service is an effective learning experience for developing students' leadership skills.

To accomplish change, you must work with other individuals (in groups) and groups of individuals (in coalitions). Change agents are leaders committed to social justice beyond their own organization, to building trans-organizational coalitions for collective action. While you may think of politicians, civil servants, researchers, and opinion leaders as leading change efforts at the community or societal level, as a student, you and others at the grass roots have an opportunity to influence large-scale social change through coalitions.

As a student engaged in community service as a change-making strategy, you may be drawn to advocate for systemic change related to your issue of concern. You are encouraged to move from passion about direct action to the development of communication strategies for social justice advocacy and civic engagement.

Appreciate Inquiry (AI), another strategy for change, is a participative process whereby you can work to identify what is right in an organization, and to leverage these positive, life-giving forces to create provocative propositions for innovation and change.

> Learning Outcomes

- To describe the Social Change Model and understand the reciprocal interaction between the three value-based perspective levels described in the model.
- To articulate how the model relates to your personal leadership experiences.
- To identify coalition building practices and develop awareness of the ways of making change.
- To learn about communication strategies for social justice advocacy and reflect upon your own preferred communication strategies for change.
- To discover the power of perspective taking and its contribution to eliciting positive moments.
- To experience the power of stories to create images of a desired future.

Strategies for Change

Activity 1: Social Change Model of Leadership

The Social Change Model of Leadership is a powerful model for understanding how collaborative leadership happens in the pursuit of change.

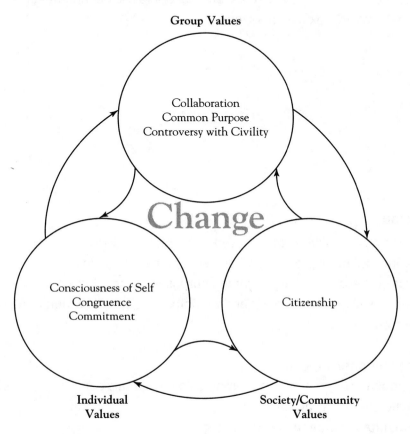

For each value of the SCM, read the description and answer the associated questions:

Collaboration

Collaboration is a central value in the model that views leadership as a group process. It increases group effectiveness because it capitalizes on the multiple talents and perspectives of each group member, using the power of that diversity to generate creative solutions and actions.

Collaboration underscores the model's relational focus. Collaboration is about human relationships, about achieving common goals by sharing responsibility, authority, and accountability. It is leadership for service.

- Why is collaboration important?
- What might be the negative impacts of a group not operating collaboratively?
- What does collaboration look like in a group?

Common Purpose

A common purpose develops when people work with others within a shared set of aims and values. Shared aims facilitate group members' engagement in collective analysis of the issues and the task to be undertaken. Common purpose is best achieved when all members of the group build and share in the vision and participate actively in articulating the purpose and goals of the group work.

- Why is common purpose important?
- What might happen to a group whose members do not share a common purpose? (be more specific than the group may dissolve!)
- How can you facilitate common purpose in a group?

Controversy with Civility

Controversy with civility recognizes two fundamental realities of any group effort: first, that differences in viewpoint are inevitable and valuable, and, second, that such differences must be aired openly and with respect and courtesy. Disagreements are inherent in almost any social interaction or group process. They bring valuable perspectives and information to the collaborative group, but eventually, they must be resolved. Such resolution is accomplished through open and honest dialogue backed by the group's commitment to understand the sources of the disagreement and to work cooperatively toward common solutions.

- What does controversy *without* civility look like?
- What does controversy with civility look like?
- What may happen to a group whose members do not handle controversy with civility?
- Why is controversy important? Why wouldn't you just try to avoid it completely?

Consciousness of Self

Consciousness of self means knowledge of yourself, or simply self-awareness. It is awareness of the values, emotions, attitudes, and beliefs that motivate one to take action. A person with a highly developed capacity for consciousness of self not only has a reasonably accurate self-concept but also is a good observer of his or her own behavior and state of mind at any given time. Consciousness of self is a fundamental value in the Social Change Model of Leadership because it constitutes the necessary condition for realizing all the other values in the model.

- Why is it important to pay attention to your consciousness of self?
- How can one improve his or her consciousness of self?
- Do you know yourself? Do you know yourself well?

Congruence

Congruence is thinking, feeling, and behaving with consistency, genuineness, authenticity and honesty toward others. Congruent persons are those whose actions are consistent with their most deeply held beliefs and convictions. Being clear about one's values, beliefs, strengths, and limitations, who one is as an individual, is essential.

- Why is congruence important?
- Have you ever behaved in a group or a team with inconsistency? Why? What is the risk of behaving with inconsistency, with the lack of genuineness or authenticity?
- One can experience a strong pressure on expressing her or his values and beliefs while working in a group or a team. What can one do to resist such pressure?

Commitment

Commitment implies intensity and duration in relation to a person, idea, or activity. It requires a significant involvement and investment of self in the object of commitment and in the intended outcomes. It is the energy that drives the collective effort. Commitment is essential to accomplishing change. It is the heart, the profound passion that drives one to action. Commitment originates from within. No one can force a person to commit to something, but organizations and colleagues can create and support an environment that resonates with each individual's heart and passions.

- Why is commitment important?
- Think about the commitment of the people in an organization you are involved with, or about the commitment in a relationship you are involved in. Starting today, what can you do to improve this commitment?
- What can teachers and students in a class do to improve their mutual commitment to the success of the class?

Citizenship

Citizenship names the process whereby the self is responsibly connected to the environment and the community. It acknowledges the interdependence of all involved in the leadership effort.

Citizenship thus recognizes that effective democracy requires individual responsibility as well as individual rights. Citizenship, in the context of the Social Change Model, means more than membership; it implies active engagement of the individual and the leadership group in an effort to serve the community. It implies social or civic responsibility. It is, in short, the value of caring about others.

- Can you explain the concept of citizenship using real-life examples?
- What are the communities you feel part of? How can you be active citizens of these communities?
- Why is citizenship important?

Arrows

The model purposefully includes arrows connecting each set of values. Answer the following questions about these connections:

How does the development of the individual values impact the development of the group values? How does the development of the group values impact the development of the individual values?

How does the development of the individual values impact the development of the societal values?

How does the development of the societal values impact the development of the individual values?

How does the development of the group values impact the development of the societal values?

How does the development of the societal values impact the development of the group values?

Change

The concept of change and strategies for change have been previously explored in this workbook, but it is important to note here that change is at the heart of the Social Change Model. Why do you think change is central to collaborative leadership? Can leadership be divorced from the concept of change?

Strategies for Change

Activity 2: Social Justice Advocacy

Read over these five communication styles for social justice advocacy.

Radvocate

- Ideas are in the extreme ends of the ideological continuum
- Helps get to the roots of issues
- Offers solid analysis
- "Voice crying out in the desert"
- Can appear self-righteous

Madvocate

- Operates from anger, indignation, moral outrage
- Shocks people out of lethargy and into awareness and action
- Can silence those who think differently
- May create enemies, not allies

Sadvocate

- Convinces through sad, subjective self-disclosures
- Can invite empathy and compassion
- Rather than rally to action, this may evoke a sense of pity and victimization

Fadvocate

- Excited about the cause du jour
- Keeps others educated about current issues
- Scant commitment to long-term engagement

Gladvocate

- Teaches through invitation, generosity
- Calls people together to listen and grow in understanding
- Tenuous tenacity—committed, yet open to dialogue
- Helps discover overlapping agendas and action items

Personal Qualities Associated with Gladvocacy

- Humility—attribute the best motive to others in their actions and words
- Faith—confidence that what others say is valuable for me to hear
- Self-denial—surrender ourselves to the possibility of changing/expanding our perspectives
- Charity—exercise generosity, fairness, affection

Adapted from Nash, R. J. (2010, May-June). What is the best way to be a social justice advocate? Communication strategies for effective social justice advocacy. *About Campus, 15*, 11–18.

What do you think of these approaches? Do you feel one is more effective than the others? Which have you seen yourself doing?

Strategies for Change

Activity 3: Narrowing Your Passions and Building Coalitions

Take 10 minutes to answer the following set of questions aimed to aid in a more advanced definition of your passions.

About what issues are you the most passionate? Which do you care about the most?

Who is affected by the issue?

Are you willing to take the time and make the sacrifices to work on this issue?

Are you willing to face the challenges associated with this issue?

Who are the shareholders or stakeholders who might join you in working with this issue?

Who is in a position to exert influence—positively or negatively—on the issue?

Who else might be interested in this project? What other individuals or organizations might you contact?

How can core participants once identified, be motivated to join the collective effort?

What do you want to accomplish? Be able to state clearly and succinctly what you are trying to do. Try explaining this to someone who knows nothing about the particular topic or area. This will force you to state things in simple terms that are easy to understand.

Where can you begin? What person or office should you contact first? The key thing is to begin—starting any project may be frustrating at first.

Strategies for Change

Activity 4: Headlines

After you have brainstormed about the issue areas that you find most salient in your life, write a single statement below in the form of a newspaper headline that relates to what you wish to accomplish in tackling your passion.

Think of recent newspaper headlines as examples—think of this as the one sentence news bullet that you would want to see printed as the headline of *The New York Times* or *The Washington Post* when your change process is completed. For example, a headline might read "College Graduate Cures Cancer with Help of Professor."

Write your headline here:

Why is this your headline? Are you actively thinking about or working on this issue? Is this connected to the passion issues you identified previously?

Strategies for Change

Activity 5: Words Create Worlds

Listed below are a range of professions. Look around the room you are sitting in, taking note of what you notice from the perspective of each profession.

For example, what assets are present in the room that would benefit the activities of people in each profession (a window for a burglar to break to enter the room)? In what ways do elements in the room present problems (electric outlets the childcare planner will need to cover)?

Profession	Observations
Child care provider	
Event planner	
Burglar	
Fire marshal	
Custodian	
Emergency shelter provider	
Account manager	
Other:	
Other:	

Now, reflect on the following questions:

How did adopting a particular profession or role shape what you noticed or perceived in the room?

Aside from professions, what other roles, identities, or perspectives shape how we perceive the world?

How does perception affect interpretation and action?

How might choosing to adopt a positive or appreciative lens change how a person views a situation?

Strategies for Change

Activity 6: The Power of Stories

This activity will require you to find another student with whom to partner. You will be conducting a 15-minute interview using the Appreciative Interview Guide provided below. Feel free to adapt this template for your specific purposes and circumstances. While your partner is answering the questions, you should record notes about themes and stories discussed, and any significant quotes. After 15 minutes have elapsed, switch roles and have your partner interview you and take notes.

Appreciative Interview Guide / Template

1. **Best Experience**. Tell me a story about the best time you have had with your organization (or team, family, class, community, or other group). Reflecting on your entire experience with that group, recall a time when you felt most alive or excited about your involvement. Describe the event in detail. Over what period of time did it take place? How did it happen? Who else was involved? What made it an exciting or transformative experience?
2. **Values**. Let's discuss some things that you value deeply. Specifically, the things you value about yourself, your work, and your organization.
   - Without being humble, what do you most value about yourself (as a person, as a member of your group or organization, as a friend, and so on)?
   - When you are feeling your best about your work (school work, group work, and so forth), what about the task itself do you value?
   - What is it about your organization (class, team, family, group, community) that you value? What is the single most important thing this group has contributed to your life (or to your learning)?
3. **Life-Giving Forces**. What do you experience as the core value of your organization (class, team, family, group, community)? Give some examples of how you experience these values. What would you like this core value to be? How will you help the group develop this core value?
4. **Three Wishes**. If you had three wishes for your organization, what would they be?

After both interviews, discuss the following questions with your partner:

- Do you find the appreciative approaches come naturally to you? Why or why not?
- What was the most "life-giving" moment of the interview for you as a listener?
- Did any particularly creative or innovative examples emerge from the interview?
- How did sharing positive stories and aspirations for success affect your energy for change?
- What excites or worries you about adopting more asset-based approaches to yourself and your work?

AI interview template adapted from www.CenterforAppreciativeInquiry.net

❯ Reflection Questions for Further Exploration

- Revisit the Social Change Model. What personal values guide your leadership? How does your thinking, feeling, and behaving around these values show congruence? How do you demonstrate your commitment to those values?

- Again, consider the Social Change Model as it relates to an organization in which you are a participant. What happens when you are faced with a difficult issue? How do you demonstrate "controversy with civility"? How might your organization improve in this area?

- Consider a recent change you have made or tried to make within an organization. What role did conflict play in this change process? Who was involved in the conflict? What did you try that was unsuccessful in working with the conflict? What was successful?

- Being an effective change agent means knowing key decision makers within the community. What campus officials do you need to know better? How might you go about becoming better acquainted with them?

❯ Reference

Nash, R. J. (2010). What is the best way to be a social justice advocate? Communication strategies for effective social justice advocacy. *About Campus, 15,* 11–19. doi: 10.1002/abc.20017

CHAPTER 12

Thriving Together

◇

> Focus of Chapter

The Relational Leadership Model focuses on a leader's ability to cultivate positive relationships. Additional models from positive psychology provide background and application for developing positive relationships and for widening the view of what it means, for you as a leader, to create a positive, productive, engaging environment. In order for you to understand what it means to engage as a positive leader focused on a flourishing environment, you must first build self-awareness around your own well-being and positivity.

Self-renewal is important both for leadership development and for development of the spirit. Stress, being unbalanced, exhaustion, and feeling overwhelmed are likely to detract from leader effectiveness. You can engage in personal renewal as a proactive strategy by trying new things, realizing that what you do matters, keeping personal balance, making time for reflection and centering, maintaining positive relationships, and prioritizing tasks. Spiritual renewal involves leading from values, meaning and purpose, and being connected to the world.

> Learning Outcomes

- To consider how well-being and positivity lead to productive, happy environments.
- To assess your own levels of well-being.
- To learn about the concept of self-renewal and how it may apply to you.
- To explore ways of generating your own self-renewal.

Thriving Together

Activity 1: Well-Being Worksheet

Martin Seligman (2011) proposes a model with five measurable dimensions that contribute to human flourishing and thriving called PERMA (p. 24). The five PERMA dimensions are charted below. For each of the five dimensions, rate yourself on a scale of zero to five, five being the highest or best. In the middle of the "pie" for each dimension, draw a dot for the numerical rating you have given yourself. Once you have drawn the five dots, connect them, creating a five-sided shape within the chart.

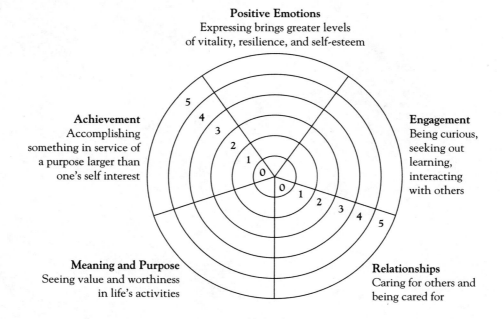

What do you notice about your well-being shape? Is it what you thought the shape would look like? Are there areas where you wish your well-being is higher? In the space below, reflect on your well-being shape.

Thriving Together

Activity 2: Reflect on Renewal and Balance

Answer the following questions:

How well are you eating?

How much sleep do you get?

Do you exercise or are you engaged in physical activity on a regular basis? Describe your exercise regimen.

How much of your time do you spend doing things that "fill your tanks"—things you really enjoy and get a positive charge from? What kinds of things do you do?

How much stress do you have in your life, and what do you do to manage the stress?

Think about what you have just written. What are common threads that emerge?

Thriving Together

Activity 3: Savoring the Good

Think of something good that has happened in the past 12, 24, 36 hours. It does not have to be something big, but can be. Take in the experience and focus on the positive aspects of it as well as the positive emotions connected to it.

Hold yourself there for 30 seconds and imagine the feel-good experience soaking into your body.

What was that experience life for you? How often do you think about the good things that happen to you?
What sources of renewal can you find on your campus? Be specific.
(Adapted from Hanson, 2009)

Thriving Together

Activity 4: Creating a Spiritual Development Plan

Astin, Astin, and Lindholm (2011, p. 4) define spirituality as having "... to do with the values that we hold most dear, our sense of who we are and where we come from, our beliefs about why we are here—the meaning and purpose that we see in our work and our life—and our sense of connectedness to one another and to the world around us."

The authors measured spiritual development through measures of equanimity, ecumenical worldview, ethic of caring, charitable involvement, and spiritual quest. They found that the most beneficial means of students developing spiritually is to engage in the following activities:

- Service learning: taking courses that involve engaging with nonprofit and community organizations.
- Volunteer work: volunteering time for a charity or service organization.
- Studying abroad: spending a semester outside of the United States in an academic program for credit.
- Exploring spiritual traditions: joining a spiritual community, being part of an organization exploring spirituality, or taking classes that involve reading sacred texts and discussion spiritual traditions.
- Engaging in contemplative practices: engaging in a regular practice such as yoga, meditation, tai chi, qigong, prayer, or practices that are similarly contemplative.

Create a plan detailing how you will engage with at least three of the areas during your college career. The purpose of this assignment is for you to create intentions around developing your spirit, which is a source of long-term renewal.

> Reflection Questions for Further Exploration

- Identify examples of individuals in your organization who are negative energizers. What impact do they have on the group? Identify examples of positive energizers. What impact do they have on the group? How can you maximize the contributions of positive energizers?

- The title of this chapter is, Thriving Together. What would your organization or university look like if it was *thriving together*?

- Think of an individual who you would identify as a resonant leader. Someone who is mindful, hopeful, and compassionate and who intentionally seeks ways to stay renewed. What does this person do that brings resonance to others and to himself or herself? (If possible, arrange an interview to ask questions to explore this.)

- What self-renewal strategies or techniques can you use to reach your full potential in life or in your leadership?

> References

Astin, A. W., Astin, H. S., & Lindholm, J. A. (2010). *Cultivating the spirit: How college can enhance students' inner lives.* San Francisco, CA: Jossey-Bass.

Hanson, R. (2009). *Buddha's brain: The practical neuroscience of happiness, love, and wisdom.* Oakland, CA: New Harbinger Publications, Inc.

Seligman, M.E.P. (2011). *Flourish: A visionary new understanding of happiness and well-being.* New York, NY: Free Press

FINAL THOUGHTS

Each chapter in the book ended with a series of reflection questions, many of which have been included in this workbook. As you continue your journey in exploring leadership, consider these final questions:

How have you been able to apply what you have learned about leadership?

How are you more aware of yourself?

What things do you now see differently? How are you changing?

How will you continue your learning about leadership?

What is your own philosophy of leadership?

What purpose does your leadership serve?

How can you see the goodness in others?

How can you bring out the best in others and maximize their strengths?

What does it look like and feel like when you are able to do what you are best at doing on a regular basis?

Her Mother's Daughter

Evie Grace was born in Kent, and one of her earliest memories is of picking cherries with her grandfather who managed a fruit farm near Selling. Holidays spent in the Kent countryside and the stories passed down through her family inspired her to write her Maids of Kent trilogy.

Evie now lives in Devon with her partner and dog. She has a grown-up daughter and son.

She loves researching the history of the nineteenth century and is very grateful for the invention of the washing machine, having discovered how the Victorians struggled to do their laundry.

Her Mother's Daughter is Evie's second novel in the trilogy, following on from *Half a Sixpence*. The third and final novel is out July 2018.

Also by Evie Grace

Half a Sixpence